FRIEDRICH DÜRRENMATT

Modern Literature Monographs

❖❖

FRIEDRICH DÜRRENMATT

Armin Arnold

Frederick Ungar Publishing Co.
New York

Translated from the original German and revised, with new material, by the author with Sheila Johnson. Published by arrangement with Colloquium Verlag, Berlin.

Copyright © 1972 by
Frederick Ungar Publishing Co., Inc.
Printed in the United States of America
Library of Congress Catalog Card Number: 78-178169
ISBN: 0-8044-2000-9 (cloth)

Contents

Chronology

1921: Is born on January 5, in Konolfingen (Switzerland), the son of Reinhold Dürrenmatt, a Protestant pastor, and Hulda Dürrenmatt-Zimmermann.

1935: Moves to Bern (father is chaplain at the Salemspital).

1941: Graduates from the Humboldtianum (high school) in Bern.

1941–42: Studies literature and philosophy in Zurich.

1942: Continues studies at the University of Bern.

1943: Makes first attempts at writing: the unpublished *Komödie* and several prose sketches. Produces paintings and drawings.

1945: First narrative work, "Der Alte" [The Old Man], is published in the Bern newspaper *Der Bund*.

1946–48: Lives in Basel.

1947: Marries Lotti Geissler. First performance of *Es steht geschrieben* takes place on April 19 (Zurich).

1948: *Der Blinde* is performed on January 10 (Basel).

1948–52: The Dürrenmatts live in Ligerz on Lake Biel.

1949: *Romulus the Great* is performed on April 25 (Basel).

1950: First detective novel, *The Judge and His Hangman*, appears in installments in *Der Beobachter*.

1952: Purchases a house in Neuchâtel, where he and his family (wife and three children) still live today; *The Marriage of Mr. Mississippi* is produced on March 26 (Munich).

1953: *An Angel Comes to Babylon* is performed on December 22 (Munich).

1956: *The Visit* is produced on January 29 (Zurich).

1957: Completes first film script: *Es geschah am hellichten Tag.*

1959: *Frank der Fünfte* is produced on March 19 (Zurich).

1962: *The Physicists* is produced on February 20 (Zurich). Gore Vidal's adaptation of *Romulus the Great* is produced in New York.

1963: First performance of *Herkules und der Stall des Augias* takes place on March 20 (Zurich).

1966: *Der Meteor* is performed on January 20 (Zurich).

1967: *Die Wiedertäufer* is produced on March 16 (Zurich).

1968: *König Johann* is produced on September 18 (Basel).

1969: First performance of *Play Strindberg* takes place on February 8 (Basel). Travels to America.

1970: Three plays receive first performances: *Urfaust* in Zurich (October); *Portrait eines Planeten* (November) and *Titus Andronicus* (December), both in Düsseldorf.

1971: Dürrenmatt celebrates fiftieth birthday; publishes the short novel *Der Sturz.*

1

*The Horror
Lurking
Behind
the Scenes*

"I am no small-town author," Dürrenmatt has said. "But the village produced me; so I am still a slow-talking villager, not a city person—least of all a big-city person—even though I probably couldn't live in a village any more."[1] Dürrenmatt's native village, Konolfingen, is in the Swiss canton of Bern, not far from Langnau, the center of the Emmenthaler cheese industry.

Friedrich Dürrenmatt was born on January 5, 1921. His father, Reinhold, was a Protestant pastor in Konolfingen since 1911. When Friedrich was five years old, a two-volume work about his grandfather was published—*Ulrich Dürrenmatt und seine Gedichte: ein Stück Literatur- und Schweizergeschichte* [Ulrich Dürrenmatt and His Poems: A Chapter in the History of Literature and the History of Switzerland], by J. Howald. Ulrich Dürrenmatt (1849–1908) was the son of a farmer in Guggisberg. He became a teacher and married Anna Maria Breit from Steffisburg, who was also a teacher. After having taught in his home district, Ulrich Dürrenmatt was transferred to several other posts. Four years later he gave up his position as teacher to assume the editorship of the *Berner Volkszeitung* [Bern People's Journal], a newspaper that was published in Herzogenbuchsee.

Ulrich Dürrenmatt underwent a development similar to that of the important Swiss writer Jeremias Gotthelf. A radical young man at first, he evolved into a conservative who fought with vehemence against liberalism and socialism. He was a man of extraordinary intelligence and flawless character. He was elected first to the district legislature in the canton of Bern and then to the National Assembly, where he exercised great influence upon the politics of Bern and of Switzerland. His newspaper regularly carried an editorial—in the form of a poem.

Howald made a comprehensive selection from the 2500 extant poems of Ulrich Dürrenmatt. Almost all, whether written in standard German, dialect, or a French-German hybrid, possess penetrating force. One can understand why Ulrich Dürrenmatt was so much feared by his opponents and admired by his grandson. Friedrich Dürrenmatt, says his biographer Hans Bän-ziger, knows many of Ulrich's poems by heart.

Because Ulrich Dürrenmatt was also a religious man, it is not surprising that his son Reinhold studied theology. Another son of Ulrich Dürrenmatt's became a minister in the government in Bern, and his son—that is, Friedrich's cousin—became a member of the National Assembly, as well as editor-in-chief of a leading Swiss newspaper, the *Basler Nachrichten* [Basel News]. Ulrich Dürrenmatt had, by the way, discovered the law of bureaucratic propagation long before Parkinson: "The greatest impetus to increase bureaucratic positions is produced by the compulsive lawmaking of the governing body. Lawmaking and bureaucracy work hand in hand. Every new law produces new officials, and every new official commands the raw material necessary to put through new laws."[2]

In 1935 Dürrenmatt's father became chaplain at the Salem Hospital in Bern. Friedrich attended the Freies Gymnasium for two and a half years, then the Humboldtianum (another high school), where he successfully completed his high-school work and received his diploma in 1941. This period is said to have been the darkest time of his life. After this, he began to study German literature, philosophy, and the natural sciences —first at the University of Zurich, then at the University of Bern.

In the short story "Der Tunnel" [The Tunnel] (in the volume *Die Stadt* [The City]) there is a student who boards the express train to Zurich on a Sunday evening (Departure: Bern, 17:50; Arrival: Zurich, 19:27). The city of Bern is never mentioned by name; rather, it is designated as "hometown." The story consists—among other things—of a portrait of the student, who resembles Dürrenmatt. He describes himself in this manner:

A twenty-four year old who had purposely made himself fat because he wanted a protective insulation against the horror that he saw lurking behind the scenes (his ability to perceive this horror was his talent, perhaps his only one). He chose also to plug up the orifices in his flesh, since it was these very holes through which that monstrosity could rush in. He plugged them up by smoking cigars (Ormond Brazil 10), wearing a second pair of glasses—sunglasses—over the first, and stuffing wads of cotton in his ears.[3]

"To see the horror behind the scenes"—one could take this as a motto for Dürrenmatt's early works. On October 2, 1943, he completed a play, *Komödie* [Comedy], which has never been published. According to Hans Bänziger, it consists of a series of "monstrous fantasies of hell, with whores, drunkards, technicians, maimed people. . . ."[4] A powerful machine of destruction is built. Finally, everything ends in an explosion. One scene of *Komödie* is dedicated to the memory of Kafka. It is certain that the young Dürrenmatt knew *The Trial, The Castle*, and most of Kafka's tales.

Only a few works Dürrenmatt wrote in the forties have been published. At that time he intended to become a painter. Nonetheless, Dürrenmatt did write sketches for literary cabarets, theater reviews for the weekly *Die Weltwoche* [World Week], and detective stories for *Der Beobachter* [Observer], then Switzerland's most popular periodical. In addition, a broadcasting station commissioned him to write some radio plays. Almost all of Dürrenmatt's early work was written for one purpose only—to make money. The only exceptions were some early narrative pieces later collected in the volume *Die Stadt*. These were the first tortuous steps of an author who was still feeling his way. No one knew that better than Dürrenmatt himself, who wrote in the epilogue to *Die Stadt*: "This work is not an attempt to establish values or to tell some stories; rather, it is a necessary attempt to fight out something with myself. . . ."5

Hans Bänziger does not think very highly of the early fiction. Elisabeth Brock-Sulzer, another Swiss critic, finds, on the contrary, that several of the short pieces are among the best writings of Dürrenmatt. In any case, the stories in *Die Stadt* form the nucleus out of which the subsequent works grew. They illustrate Dürrenmatt's intellectual and emotional state at the beginning of his career. The book, therefore, deserves careful examination.

The first piece, "Weihnacht" [Christmas], written in 1943, is only a half page long. The story is told in the first person and consists of twenty-eight short sentences and fragments:

It was Christmas. I was walking across the wide plain. The snow was like glass. It was cold. The air was dead. Not a movement, not a sound. The horizon was round. The heavens black. The stars dead. The moon borne yesterday to her grave. The sun not risen. I cried out. I did not hear myself. I cried out again. I saw a body lying on the snow. It was the Christ child. The limbs white and rigid. The halo a frozen yellow plate. I took the child into my hands. I moved his hands up and down. I opened his eyelids. He had no eyes. I was hungry. I ate the halo. It tasted like stale bread. I bit his head off. Old marzipan. I walked on.6

This sketch has a familiar sound. The repeated cry reminds one of certain expressionists who were gripped in a similar way by the horror of the suddenly discovered reality of life. Dürrenmatt's resemblance to Kafka is more pronounced in other sketches. But we *are* reminded of the grandmother's fairy tale in Büchner's *Woyzeck*. The "poor girl" on her way to heaven is disappointed by each phenomenon she encounters: by the moon, which is a "chunk of rotten wood"; by the sun, which is "a wilted sunflower"; and by the stars, which are nothing but "little gold mosquitoes." Finally, she sees that the Earth is nothing but a chamber pot upon which she sits down, bereft of hope.

The narrator of "Weihnacht" is in a similar situation. He, too, has recognized the nothingness of sun, moon, and stars. The image of the cold, snow-covered Earth with its dead air, which no longer carries any sound, has a considerably more gruesome effect than Büchner's "chamber pot." Having established that the Earth is worth nothing, Büchner stops. Dürrenmatt, on the other hand, takes up his central theme at this very point. It is Christmas, the day of Christ's birth. The narrator finds the Christ child in the snow. Has the real Christ child frozen to death? Or is it a doll or perhaps a marzipan figure such as one might buy at a bakery? Certainly, the narrator is disillusioned by religion: the halo tastes like stale bread; the body, like old marzipan. Is that supposed to mean that Christ is dead, that the Eucharist has no significance?

No one seems to have noticed that *Die Stadt* begins on the day of Christ's birth and ends on the day of his crucifixion. (The crucifixion is seen through the eyes of Pilate, who does not for a moment doubt that Christ is a god.) God is also present in "Der Tunnel" and intervenes importantly in the action. He also figures in "Der Folterknecht" [The Torturer], the story that follows "Weihnacht." It is therefore inconsistent to conclude from "Weihnacht" that Dürrenmatt wanted to imply God is dead. "Weihnacht" is a parable about the despair of a man who becomes conscious of life's truths, who recognizes his own helplessness and weakness, and who blames God for not acting more justly toward mankind and for not giving it a better chance. This man can no longer love and trust God.

"Der Folterknecht" dates from the same year as "Weihnacht" and is written in similarly terse sentences. It consists of twenty-one paragraphs followed by a short dialogue between God and a man, and a closing sentence: "A man dies." This tale, too, transmits the despairing cry of a man who holds God responsible— since he is all-powerful—for the grim condition of humanity in general and of the individual in particular.

The first three paragraphs describe a torture chamber. It lies deep in a cellar. In the corner sits the torturer. As approaching steps of one or more people are heard, everything springs to life. An orgy of terrible human suffering breaks loose. Afterward, everything sinks back into torpidity. The story continues; the torturer enters a bar, where a stranger joins him. The latter is distinguished, rich, and comfortably married. He has seen the realities of life: "I am going to get old. I shall die. I'll rot. I'll become what you are. My life is a descent into nothingness. You never change; you are in an eternal void. You are the most fortunate of men."[7] He knows that the idea of a happy man is an illusion. The behavior of the torturer confirms his knowledge that behind man lurks "the crying animal." The stranger knows that the torturer is God. He calls him "the beginning and the end." He suggests that

they exchange their forms for two years. The torturer
agrees.

In a large, haunted chamber, swarming with bats,
the torturer and the stranger assume their new forms.
As God catches sight of his former shape (now on the
other man), he flees, horrified. He is content with the
stranger's form and with his wife, whom he also takes
as his. God resolves not to surrender his new shape.

After a time, however, the sight of a branch reminds God of pincers used in torturing; behind the plas-
ter walls of his home he perceives the stone masonry of
the cellar. Wine reminds him of blood. At the ap-
pointed hour he finds his way to the haunted chamber,
but the other one does not come. Returning home, he
becomes convinced that the bed on which his wife is
lying has turned into a torturer's block. He kills his
wife. Brought to justice, he remains silent; then he himself is taken to be tortured. Now he must bear the same
things he has put others through. At this point Dürrenmatt provides the key to his parable: "The torture
chamber is the world. The world is the torment. The
torturer is God. He torments."[8]

Dürrenmatt lets God experience in his own body
what it is like to be a man. Hence the exchange, the
horror of the torturer when he catches sight of himself.
However, God is not long content to be a man. Wine
reminds him of blood; the cry of a child reminds him of
the scream of the tortured; the white skin of the woman
tempts him to set fire to it. In his inmost being he is a
sadist. What other reason would he have to turn the
world into a torture chamber? The following dialogue
supports my conclusion:

> A man cries out:
> Why didn't you come?
> God laughs:

Why should I become human again.
A man groans:
Why do you torment me?
God laughs:
I need no shadow.[9]

When God reacts to the screams and groans with laughter, when he says that he needs no shadow, does he mean that he has given up man, whom he created in his own image? If God no longer cares about man, why then does he torment him? The tale illustrates that God is basically a sadist whose nature compels him to torture man. Even after he has taken on human form and has looked on his former self as God with horror, it takes only two years until his nature breaks through again—in sadism, in the joy of tormenting others. "Der Folterknecht" is one of the bitterest indictments of God in world literature.

Is this sketch a variation on the Faust theme, as Elisabeth Brock-Sulzer believes?[10] Maybe—but a more basic comparison is to Kafka's "In the Penal Colony." The island in Kafka's story stands for the Earth, which since Adam has been a labor camp, one in which men are punished for the sin of Adam and Eve. The penalty is death, and the machine is leading us toward this end in that it ages us and etches wrinkles in our skin. Only after the sixth hour, after life's midpoint, does man notice the way he is being toyed with. He cannot, however, escape the machine. At the twelfth hour he is thrown into the grave.

In the remaining tales in *Die Stadt*, the language is different. Dürrenmatt abandons short sentences in favor of a more realistic style, which includes long descriptive statements. "Der Hund" [The Dog] seems to be a dream vision in which a rich industrialist comes to understand the truth about the tragic situation of man on earth. He becomes a preacher and lives in poverty. From the moment he begins to preach, he is accompanied by a huge dog, who never leaves him and who later attacks him. The narrator, a young man, has an affair with the daughter of the preacher. The daughter later goes to fetch her lover so that he can help fight off the dog. But when they arrive, the animal has already torn the preacher to shreds. The police investigation uncovers neither the dog nor the daughter; the narrator, however, sees them both pass by his house.

Dürrenmatt ascribes Christ-like characteristics to the dog when he says that it walks along like "a lamb" and is only seen again "after three days." The dog, with his glowing, sulfur-yellow eyes, is the embodiment of evil; for Dürrenmatt, evil indicates God. As a symbol of God, the dog takes over the preacher's life and eventually destroys it. Like the God of the Old Testament, the dog is called by no name. Also important is the manner in which people react to the dog: the sidewalk preacher talks to men about the Word of Love; what they see, however, is the form of present evil—the dog. In other words, they cannot believe in a loving God because the very real things they experience in the world are undeniably evil.

There is something dreamlike about "Das Bild des Sisyphos" [The Picture of Sisyphus]; the narrator himself alludes to this quality. The symbolism is, however, less difficult to decipher than that of "Der Hund." A painter copies a painting by Bosch—a portrait of hell that includes Sisyphus, the man condemned, in classical mythology, to roll a rock up a hill forever. The artist sells the work to a banker for a large sum, gives up his artistic ambitions, and becomes very wealthy. If only he could regain possession of his painting now, he would prove—so he believes—that one really can make "something out of nothing." The demonstration fails because the banker refuses to return the painting. The two financially powerful opponents continue to fight until they both are impoverished: only then does the painter regain possession of his picture; and he burns it. He played Sisyphus without realizing it and lived in the hell that he had himself painted.

"Der Theaterdirektor" [The Director] is a parable of man led astray by evil. It is obvious that the theater stands for something else—Germany, perhaps. The director could be Hitler; the actress who does not adapt, who becomes ridiculous with time, and who is finally killed, would then symbolize human reason. Dürrenmatt's parallels between the crafty tactics of a dictator and the techniques of the director are excellent.

The tale "Die Falle" [The Trap] first appeared separately under the title "Der Nihilist" [The Nihilist]. The beginning and end of the story are first-person narratives, while the central part, a parable of the destruction of humanity, is depicted as a dream and is written in the third person. The nihilist, who tells the parable, views the history of mankind as it is described in the dream vision: the human race tumbles in a great mass, with closed eyes, down the stairs into hell and destruction by fire.

One man turns around at the last moment and works his way back up the stairs against the masses. He proceeds upward through the Middle Ages into antiquity, then into the Stone Age, and finally back to the beginnings of humanity. People appear less and less frequently; it gets colder and colder. He cannot bear the situation alone. He cannot keep on going; at the beginning of human history there seems to be only a great void. Finally, the man turns around again and plunges with the rest of mankind into the depths.

This is the dream that the nihilist tells to the "I" narrator of the story. The dream explains the nihilist's desire to commit suicide. He, like the man in the dream, is afraid of doing so. After telling the story, he still seeks self-destruction; he symbolically sets out for the border. A woman finds him there and leads him toward the village. He kills her, without summoning the courage to end his own life. Now he turns back from the border and enters the city again.

After he has told all of this to the narrator, he plans to kill him, because the narrator, unsuspecting, has listened to all this and could incriminate the nihilist because of the woman's murder (thus the title, "The Trap"). But the nihilist does finally manage to find the necessary courage and shoots himself.

In the epilogue to *Die Stadt* Dürrenmatt explains that his primary purpose was not to tell stories; instead, it was to break away from pure description and into philosophy. The individual parts could then be designated as philosophical parables. "Die Falle" and "Das Bild des Sisyphos" show the influence of Camus. The long sketch "Die Stadt," which forms the third part of the volume, has its source in Plato, namely in his allegory of the cave from the seventh book of the *Republic*, which Dürrenmatt refers to in his sketch. Concepts of reality and illusion are dealt with. A man (with his fellowmen) has, from birth, been chained facing the back wall of a cave. Outside, behind him, burns a bright fire, and between man and fire people pass carrying statues and other objects. The shadows these passing figures cast on the cave wall are the only images of the world that the chained man knows; consequently, he takes the shadows for reality. Or, more simply, a man who from birth sees nothing except a television screen will not be able to imagine that the image on the screen is only the shadow of reality.

Dürrenmatt's sketch seems to consist of fragments of a Kafkaesque novel that he never completed. After a description of the city of Bern, the narrator sketches his own room, which provides him with a protective shelter similar to Kafka's burrow (in the short story "Der Bau" ["The Burrow"]) for the eternally intimidated animal. In the third section, Dürrenmatt describes a rebellion of the masses against the city. This city is just as immune to attack as Kafka's castle: a lunatic's scream suffices to defend it. In the final section, the narrator himself enters into the service of the city. The three fates (or the Trinity?) direct him to a niche in a very dimly lit underground corridor where criminals are jailed. The guards—and the narrator believes himself to be such a person—are, however, indistinguishable from the prisoners.

In time, fear and despair creep into his heart. Reality and illusion blend together. Will he really be free to leave the corridor? Dare he believe that he is free? Or is this persuasion based solely on fear? The meaning of the parable is this: every human being is placed in his own dark niche. Does he have a free will or does he only imagine that he does? Does he only believe in his freedom (or in God) because otherwise fear would drive him to despair? The sketch closes with a long meditation that leads nowhere; it again reminds one of Kafka.

"Der Tunnel," written in the exact, realistic manner of Dürrenmatt's later detective stories, was the last part of *Die Stadt* to be written. The Bern–Zurich train mentioned there, with its corresponding arrival and departure times, can be found in the Swiss train schedule of the 1950s; the tunnel outside the town of Burgdorf is accurately described. The tale depicts a vision of hell, as does "Die Falle." Here, too, humanity races, blind and unguided, down into the bowels of the earth. We lose sight of the train as it dives downward on a ninety-degree course; the student answers the supervisor's question, "What is to be done?" with, "Nothing. God is letting us fall, and so we are plunging down toward him."[11]

Because of its style, "Der Tunnel" does not seem to belong to this volume. There is little of the despairing agony of the other pieces. Dürrenmatt writes here with irony and humor: the conductor never loses his conviction that the train—tunnel or not—will arrive at its usual time in Olten. The supervisor still conscientiously fills out his charts even in the face of universal perdition. And the chess player comforts himself with the statistic that Switzerland is the country with the greatest number of tunnels.

In the final sketch of the volume, "Pilatus" [Pilate], Dürrenmatt portrays the Passion on the basis of the following assumptions: Pilate knows that Jesus is a god; the crowds, however, do not know it. The Roman expects that Jesus will free himself at some point or another and will take revenge on his tormentors. He does not believe in the humility of the god "whose human form was a ruse to tempt mankind."[12] Pilate hates the fanatic masses of people. Because he sees that the god has himself taken on the dirty, ragged appearance of a man of the people, he concludes that only "in a fit of inconceivable hatred" could it have occurred "to the god to appear in this lowly disguise."[13] He believes that Jesus is intentionally allowing himself to be thus treated that he might later have a reason to kill the Jews and him, Pilate, as well. Then, as the sun grows dark, and the earth trembles, Pilate is convinced that Jesus is now taking his revenge.

Jesus appears in the story as the epitome of indifference. He does not concern himself with the masses, nor is he conscious of Pilate's conflict and terror of death. He does not even consider it worth the effort to look at the governor. At the end, the reader has more sympathy for Pilate than for the "god" who could have resisted and thereby have spared humanity and Pilate their great guilt. To Jesus, as to the torturer in "Der Folterknecht," there clings something sadomasochistic.

Because the book concludes with "Pilatus," while chronologically "Der Tunnel" belongs at the end, we can surmise that Dürrenmatt had a definite order in mind for this first volume. I have already said that it begins with the day of Christ's birth and ends with his death. Significantly, the two pieces do not describe Christ's misery and destitution. Dürrenmatt is interested in showing that man can count on neither the Christ child nor the crucified Christ. Christ has abandoned man; he does not care what happens to him; he can be dismissed as a source of comfort and hope. The tales from "Weihnacht" through "Pilatus" are parables of the despair, abandonment, and downfall of the individual man and of mankind in general. No help is to be expected from God; if he should happen to take an interest in humanity at all, then it is only as a torturer.

Dürrenmatt has never lost this pessimistic concept of the world: he has always seen "the horror lurking behind the scenes." But, with time, he has perceived and described it differently. The sketches in *Die Stadt* came into being as the result of a shock: suddenly Dürrenmatt stood without the shield of faith, face to face with human existence. Above all, he saw with horror that God—if he exists at all—is unjust. Justice and injustice, the senselessness of human existence, the "horror lurking behind the scenes"—these remain Dürrenmatt's central themes. But later he was able to treat these themes with irony; what had been horrible became grotesque.

2

The Early Dramas

Dürrenmatt wrote *Es steht geschrieben* [It Is Written] between the summer of 1945 and February, 1946, that is, at the same time he was writing most of his sketches in *Die Stadt*. It would seem strange if his world view, despairing and pessimistic in the prose volume, were different in this drama. Nonetheless, Elisabeth Brock-Sulzer considers the conclusion of the play "conciliatory." In the closing scene Knipperdollinck, who had taken Christian teachings seriously and had rid himself of all his wealth, hangs on the torturer's wheel and speaks with God:

> Lord! Lord!
> Look at me here on this wheel, with open arms,
>   ready to receive you!
> See my body, which is broken, and my limbs, which
>   are stretched upon this piece of wood;
> it embraces me, it is the ultimate test you have
>   set for me so that I might come to know myself!
> I have cast away everything, as if my possessions
>   were fire in my hands, and you have not rejected
>   any of my gifts.
> Lord! Lord!
> Now you smother me with your silence and plunge
>   the icy chill of your heavens into my heart
>   like a sword!
> My despair rises directly to you—a glowing flame;
> and the torment, which tears the very flesh from
>   my bones, rises too;
> and the cry from my lips, which reaches out to you
> and which fades away now in praise;
> for everything that happens reveals your infinity,
>   Lord!
> The depths of my despair are merely the reflection
>   of your justice,
> and my body lies on this wheel as in a chalice,
> which you now fill to the brim with your mercy![1]

Elisabeth Brock-Sulzer draws the following conclusion from the play: "It is one of the remarkable absurdities of our time that, in light of this play, one could ever fail to recognize Dürrenmatt as a thoroughly religious . . . writer. At least he was one at that particular time."[2] The author of *Es steht geschrieben* and *Die Stadt* is religious insofar as he does not ignore the idea of God. But both works seem to say that if there is a God then he is a tormentor who either tortures man with sadistic enjoyment or, at best, ignores him.

There is, however, one particular idea that has no connection with God (who may or may not exist); this is the concept of justice. God does not differentiate between right and wrong; he tortures whomever happens to fall into his hands. The Bishop expresses this clearly: "Strange that you speak of guilt and penance, Count von Hessen. What insignificant words in relation to such great misery! It is all one to man, his own actions and the wheel on which God has twisted him."[3] The philosophy is the same as that in "Der Folterknecht." When the Count calls the lives of those children who have starved in the war "meaningless," the Bishop answers, "The meaning lies within their torment, Count von Hessen."[4]

The language of the play is, in places, elevated and full of pathos. At times it reminds one of the Bible (the Psalms); and at times, it sounds like the language of expressionistic dramas such as Georg Kaiser's *Hölle Weg Erde* [Hell Way Earth] and Fritz von Unruh's *Platz* [Place]. Dürrenmatt recognizes the risk of being an epigone. So again and again he inserts words and even whole scenes in which he varies his tone: he uses Swiss dialect expressions and inserts comic couplets. Quotations taken from the classics have the effect of parody, and Bockelson, in the oriental, image-rich

language of Hadschi Halef Omar (a character created
by the German adventure-story writer Karl May), lists
a series of culinary delicacies. Mildly obscene expressions and every sort of wordplay interrupt the grander
style effectively.

The world of this drama is an insane world in
which nothing makes sense. The good Knipperdollinck
and the evil Bockelson both end on the wheel. Bockelson has had the better deal at that; in any event, he had
indulged his taste for pleasure for a while. It is best to
be a realist and a skeptic, to have no principles or at
least to throw them overboard at the right moment.
Dürrenmatt seems to have studied the Anabaptist
movement in Münster when he was planning to write a
historical dissertation. He warns, on one hand, against
drawing parallels between 1535 and 1945; on the other
hand, he believes that the world "was just the same
yesterday as it is today and as it will be tomorrow."[5]

The Swiss critics Beda Allemann and Christian
Jauslin interpret *Es steht geschrieben* as a parody. Allemann goes so far as to assert that "*Es steht geschrieben* is not an Anabaptist problem play; rather, it is a
parody of every problem play."[6] The spoken word in
the drama shows itself to be "parodied throughout."
Dürrenmatt has succeeded where Nietzsche in *Zara-
thustra* failed, in the "effortless use of Luther's German." The moving monologues of the three Anabaptists at the beginning terminate on a comical note: each
of them exits on " a note of parody." On his first entrance, Jan Matthisson mentions that he considers it his
duty "to point out that the writer of this doubtful and,
in an historical perspective, frankly insulting parody of
the Anabaptists" is nothing other

than an uprooted Protestant in the broadest sense,
    afflicted with a knot of doubt, mistrustful of the

> faith that he looks up to, because he has lost
> it,
> a pot pourri of sad clichés, who takes prurient
> pleasure in the indecent,
> who does not hesitate to turn tail
> before the pope, that mortal enemy of religion,
> just so that from this vantage point, too, he
> can again take up his all-out attack against us.[7]

Dürrenmatt apologizes to the Protestant public for letting the Bishop off so easily. Elsewhere, however, he claims that the Bishop is an unhistorical figure, that actually he had a mistress and boy lovers. Luther is shown in just as doubtful a light as the church; after all, he had sanctioned the Count's marrying two women.

To be sure, much of the drama is parody, but the despairing cry of the sketches in *Die Stadt* is echoed again and again. In contrast to *Die Stadt*, where one is for the most part directly confronted by the naked terror, this same terror is relegated to the background of *Es steht geschrieben* and is thus partly concealed. The author continually distracts the audience by means of comedy, parody, irony, grotesque action, and other devices to create detachment. Again and again it is made clear to the members of the audience that they are in a theater: with the greatest monotony, just about every important character introduces himself to the audience on his first entrance.

What sort of people are they? Egotists and visionaries. The poor guard wants to be baptized only if he can profit economically. Mollenhöck feels safe from persecution, since he is the only one who knows how to use the cannons; and all Christians need these weapons. The Bishop stands closest to the Christian principle that teaches that man does not live on Earth just to be happy. If there were a Christian God, then the sin of

the Anabaptists would lie in their conviction that they
are perfect, that is, in their pride. The Bishop is an
appealing character not so much because he is a Christian (actually he does not act like one) but because he
is a clever skeptic who knows the world around him; he
is ironic toward himself and loathes all forms of fanati-
cism.

Knipperdollinck wants to do good, but by reliev-
ing the Bishop of his debts he actually finances the
Bishop's army, and by letting Bockelson go free he
brings further misfortune upon his own family and the
city. Only when he throws his money out among the
people (as does the cashier in Georg Kaiser's *From
Morn to Midnight*) does he accidentally rescue a monk
from the executioner. But the people do not respect him
for his Christian act; on the contrary, from that point
on they no longer take him seriously.

The women in the play are not distinguished by
their intelligence or morality; they pursue the man who
is strongest at the moment, and in so doing they resemble Shaw's representatives of the "life force." Bockelson, too, is a materialist par excellence, as shown by his
answer to Mollenhöck's question about what he believes in: "In the empty heavens, in this wall, in legs
and arms, in face and hands, and in the earth which
beds down under all things like the body of a woman!
There is nothing else!"[8]

Matthisson exalts the spirit and condemns the
flesh. Bockelson, on the other hand, advocates polyg-
amy, orgies, the sensual pleasures. Both are convinced
that the kingdom of the Anabaptists is the only rightful
one and that they have been called to push through
their teachings universally, with fire and sword. Except
for the Bishop, only Judith and Knipperdollinck realize
that error and injustice are the lot of mankind.

At its first performance in Zurich the play was received with alarm, whistles, and agitation. And when they saw the dance on the roof, many in the audience left the theater in protest. One can imagine the public's confusion. It knows that Knipperdollinck is good, Bockelson bad; but then, in all friendliness, the two climb up to the roof, shortly before the destruction, and there they recite offensive proverbs. Only someone who has not taken sides and has been aware of the parody will not be angered by this scene. The dance on the roof is a grotesque provocation of the public. It symbolizes the polarities of human existence: the one dances it with "crown and scepter," the other in a "tattered shirt." Neither of the dancers is aware of his hopeless situation in life; they are both fools of God who meaninglessly and aimlessly "draw the dance of our lives to a close." And the dance ends just as senselessly as it had begun, after a "horrible cry" on the wheel, in death.

Dürrenmatt has made it a frequent practice to revise his plays. There are two, three, and even four different versions of some of the plays. He revised *Es steht geschrieben* after two decades and named the new play *Die Wiedertäufer* [The Anabaptists]. The new work was presented on March 16, 1967, in the Schauspielhaus in Zurich. Dürrenmatt has said that the new play is "the meeting of my current dramatic art with my earliest. I was tempted to run through the old play again, this time with greater awareness."[9] The text was cut and divided. In its present form, the play has two parts, twenty scenes in all.

Es steht geschrieben is the gigantic vision of a dramatist who has had little experience with the practical staging of a play. *Die Wiedertäufer* is a work by a

master of the stage, who has been through the mill. The
first version is the product of a young idealist struggling
with himself to come to terms with the horror of human
life. The second version is the product of an experi-
enced skeptic, who accepts the absurdities of life without astonishment and who no longer has illusions to
lose.

As a work for the stage, *Die Wiedertäufer* is un-
doubtedly the better work. There is more action, less
narration; the actors introduce themselves to each
other, not to the audience. The language is terser. The
monologue of Knipperdollinck on the wheel now reads
as follows:

> Lord! Lord!
> See my broken limbs, crushed by your justice
> You spread your silence over me
> You plunge your coldness into my heart
> You have not rejected any of my gifts
> Accept now as well my despair
> The torment, which tears the flesh from my bones
> The cry of my lips, which rattles in your praise
> Lord! Lord!
> My body lies on this wretched wheel as in a chalice
> Which you now fill to the brim with your mercy
> *Dies.*[10]

The biblical, psalmlike rhythm and the abundant com-
parisons have disappeared. Even punctuation at the
ends of the lines is missing.

In addition to form, the content of *Es steht geschrieben* has been greatly changed. The subtitle no
longer reads "A Drama" but "A Comedy." Bockelson
is now a playwright and actor, whom the Bishop refuses to hire and who therefore avenges himself; he is
an unsuccessful artist like Hitler. In Münster his acting
is successful, and he is not tortured on the wheel but is

taken into the service of the conquerer, the Bishop, under very favorable terms.

The role of the Bishop has taken on even greater importance. He looks on, comments, recognizes, and this time he has the final word; he realizes that everything in the world is absurd.

> The pardoned put to the wheel, the seducer pardoned
> The betrayed massacred, the victor mocked by his
>   victory
> Justice sullied by the judges
> The knot of guilt and error, of insight and wild
>   raving
> Is untied into infamy.[11]

The closing words of the ruthless Bishop are absurd coming from him (as were Knipperdollinck's):

> This inhuman world must become more humane
> But how? But how?[12]

In *Die Wiedertäufer* Dürrenmatt has increased the number of comic parts and has emphasized the political ones as well. In particular, jokes about conditions in Switzerland have been inserted. The parodies on the classical theater now sound more natural because Bockelson is an actor. The twelfth scene, in particular, calls to mind the scene in Büchner's *Leonce and Lena* in which the king is reminded of his people by a knot in his handkerchief.

One is made aware of how evil the political despots and the business magnates are and how little they concern themselves with the people. There are no idealists: even Knipperdollinck believes he is making a good deal; is he not buying his way into heaven through renunciation? The symbolic words of the vegetable hawker are made understandable to even the slowest-witted in the audience by the newly written part of the butcher.

Again the point is made that reason and humanism count for nothing in the world. As in Brecht's *Mother Courage*, war must be "rescued" for the advantage of those in power. Democracy is made fun of, too; nothing and nobody must be outstanding. For this reason, it is decided that the towers be torn down. But communism and shared property are no good either because "with them the greatest fortunes evaporate."[13]

In *Es steht geschrieben* Dürrenmatt attempted to formulate for the stage ideas he had already expressed in *Die Stadt*. The play *Die Wiedertäufer* says nothing different, but what it does say is expressed with greater refinement. It is more conventional and more amusing, but perhaps less impressive.

Der Blinde [The Blind Man], first performed on January 10, 1948, in the Basel Stadttheater, and first published in 1960, was Dürrenmatt's second play. Like *Es steht geschrieben*, it, too, belongs to the world of *Die Stadt*. The verbal style is similar to the first play, but the dramatic action is more clearly formulated. Georg Kaiser's Marke in *König Hahnrei* [King Cuckold, 1913] prefigures Dürrenmatt's title character. He pretends that he is a happy king; when anything goes wrong he simply closes his eyes and refuses to believe it. Dürrenmatt's Duke is physically blind. Unable to see, he can only believe, and in his belief he finds comfort and happiness. This Duke has been interpreted as a Job figure. But this is a Job from whom everything is taken but to whom nothing is later given back.

Along with his vision, the Duke has lost his feeling for the truth; he no longer sees reality. In order not to despair, he grasps for faith like a drowning man for a

straw. Faith is, however, only an opiate for him, because there is no just God, no basis for any hope whatever. Faith is a comforting illusion, a self-deceiving lie.

Dürrenmatt's indictment of God remains the
same: one has to be blind to be able to believe in God.
"For one who sees, there is no mercy," says Negro da
Ponte. To have faith means "to surrender yourself to
blindness." Negro is not a devil—the devil exists no
more than does God—but a realist, a skeptic, a man
without illusions, like the Bishop in *Es steht geschrieben*. He is inclined toward sadism, however, as
are several characters in *Die Stadt*.

Negro knows that the heavens are "without
mercy," and he can only laugh when the Duke expresses the following opinions: "To us much mercy has
been granted"; "Man was given both good and bad,
mercy and curse." Negro says of the blind man: "What
he does is an illusion, and what he believes is an illusion." "Faith is blessedness," says Palamedes, the blind
man's son. He asks the writer, Gnadenbrot Suppe
[Charity-Bread Soup], the familiar question: "Is God
just or unjust?" Suppe chooses the second. Whoever
believes in God is "a fool," says Palamedes.[14]

Who is this blind Duke? The play is a parable of
man's situation, as are Kafka's *The Trial* and *The Castle*. The blind one is he who closes his eyes in the face
of reality and believes in God, his grace, and his para-
dise. His blindness shields him from the horror of reality. The Duke became blind as he convalesced from an
illness, from the illness of seeing the truth and being
drawn into despair. The son of the blind man cannot
close his eyes to the horror of life. For him, the world is
hell; he has succumbed to the horror. Negro da Ponte
and his mob are best suited for life; they are skeptics,
mockers, sadists. In the world of this play, the more

inhumane a man is, the better he gets along in life.

The realm of the philosophically grotesque and absurd takes over when the blind father, himself betrayed, condemns his own innocent son and when this son makes no attempt to defend himself. Palamedes at this point expresses his own despair at life's reality: "My despair is as great as your blindness. You have completely surrendered yourself to your night, and I have given myself wholly over to my despair. Your faith has made you blind, and it has driven me to despair."[15] To the people he says:

> Through the judgment rendered on me, you will see
>   what man's faith is:
> An illusion, which this creature must fashion for
>   himself lest he despair.[16]

While Palamedes leaves his father to his comforting illusions, Negro, because of his own cynicism, decides to compel the Duke to face reality: "Why is it that those who know the most suffer, and why is it that the fool alone does not despair?"[17] But he has as little success as Gnadenbrot Suppe: the Duke does not want to know the truth, "which comes from man," because surely truth is "poison" and brings with it "despair." The Duke strangles the poet before the latter is able to tell the truth. Negro's attempt at enlightenment fails. He wants to convince the Duke that his daughter, Octavia, is alive and is his (Negro's) mistress. The Duke does not believe him. In fact, Octavia is dead; her corpse is being carried on to the stage. Thus, Negro has erred and the blind man has been right—for once.

Because the scene closes with Negro leaving the Duke with the latter's faith intact, it has often been concluded that faith wins the final victory and that, therefore, Dürrenmatt must be on the side of the believing Christian. This is nonsense. Negro is clearly right when he says, "Your faith has killed your son and your daughter."[18] The Duke's reaffirmation of faith is false: "The man who believes conquers death." He ought to say: He who believes can reconcile himself to life, because he has chosen to live not in reality but in illusion. Negro leaves the Duke behind a defeated man, but the final sentence is so ironic that it can confuse only superficial readers of the play. "So go from me then in the name of God," says the Duke, who has just strangled the poet.[19]

Der Blinde may be interpreted biographically. The blindly trusting Duke suggests Dürrenmatt's father, the Christian pastor. Aspects of Friedrich's own personality can be found in two characters: Palamedes, who has lost his faith through his exposure to cruel reality; and the penniless poet Gnadenbrot Suppe, who is finally strangled by the Duke.

3

*From
Romulus
to
The Visit*

In the fifteen months between the first performance of *Der Blinde* and that of *Romulus der Grosse* (*Romulus the Great*) on April 25, 1949, in Basel, Dürrenmatt seems to have become a completely different person. Romulus, at first glance, has scarcely anything in common with the earlier works. Initially a disciple of Kierkegaard, Dürrenmatt evolved into a Spengler with the humor of Parkinson. Dürrenmatt says nothing further of God. As before, the world is full of evil. God, however, is no longer blamed for it; instead, man, human nature, and chance are held responsible.

Alongside this change in intellectual approach there is a comparable change in language and stage technique. For the first time the characters are defined by means of language. While formerly one or the other of the characters shocked the public by occasionally throwing in a bit of jargon or dialect, now the figures speak within well-defined limits. The German critic Hans-Jürgen Syberberg has explored the differences among the cultivated language of Romulus, his family, and Emilian; the business jargon of the traders Apollonius and Caesar Rupf; and, finally, the bureaucratic language of the court officials and servants.

Instead of achieving critical distance through the whimsical and random use of jargon or dialect, Dürrenmatt secures detachment through the intrusion of such characters as Caesar Rupf and Apollonius. The audience, of course, knows that these types are as clearly out of place in the fifth century as is the twentieth-century businessmen's language they speak. Again and again the audience is disillusioned. It knows that things are happening on stage that do not belong to fifth century Roman life; therefore, parallels must be drawn with the present. Furthermore, the audience can never forget that it is in a theater.

The action of the play takes place between break-
fast on March 15 and the same meal on March 16, in
the year 476 A.D. at the villa of the Caesar Romulus in
Campania. Dürrenmatt observes the unities of time and
place. There are historical associations evoked by just
the title of the play: Romulus was the final, decadent
Caesar of Rome. In his reign the once-proud Roman
Empire fell into the hands of the barbarians; culture
and science were annihilated. Roman civilization was
followed by a thousand years of what is popularly
called the Dark Ages, a period of witch hunting, super-
stition, and widespread illiteracy.

Romulus would seem a figure made for a tragedy.
In Dürrenmatt, however, nothing happens the way one
would imagine. To be sure, at the very beginning a
messenger appears with terrible news; but the mood,
which one might have expected to be tense and tragic,
is immediately destroyed by the sound of cackling hens;
Romulus's villa is a chicken farm. It immediately becomes clear that the fall of an empire will be treated in
comic terms. Romulus himself articulates this attitude:
"For anyone who is standing on the brink of disaster
like us, there is only one comprehensible thing left—
comedy."[1]

In its early versions the play was sometimes
strained in its logic. As the Germanic leaders appear
before Romulus, he is able to win them over, one by
one, by making them governors and raising them into
the nobility. Odoaker is taken prisoner by Caesar and
appoints Romulus emperor of the Germanic people.
Romulus, however, resigns within minutes and names
Odoaker ruler of Italy, after which he cheerfully retires
to private life.

Only in the second version did it occur to Dürrenmatt to provide a reason for Romulus's obvious idle-

ness. Romulus has, from the beginning, intended to destroy the Roman Empire. Why? Rome "knew the truth
but she chose power; she knew humanity but she chose
tyranny."[2] The idealistic Romulus could best over-
throw the empire by becoming her Caesar. To accomplish this, he married Julia. And for twenty years he
has remained passive, has not supported the armies,
and has allowed the empire to drift into bankruptcy.
For this reason the Germans were able to conquer Italy
so easily. To Julia's mind, Romulus (when he explains
his behavior) is a traitor. He disagrees: "No, I am
Rome's judge." This arrogance is somewhat mitigated
in that he is prepared to perish personally with the
empire. He forgoes his chance to escape and expects
the Germans to kill him. It is one of life's ironies that
his wife and daughter drown on their flight to Sicily
while he receives a pension from Odoaker.

Romulus is at first a puzzle: he appears stupid,
lazy, and incompetent—a dullard who has no concep-
tion of what is going on around him. He is witty, to be
sure; but at the end of Act I one tends to agree with the
messenger who cries out, "Rome has a disgraceful
Caesar!" Only in the third act, when he is confronted
by several persons who want to murder him in the interest of the empire, does he win our respect and sympathy. At this point we acknowledge that Romulus has
greater depth than we had thought. When Emilian plans
to bring out a toast on justice, Romulus responds, "Justice is a terrible thing, Emilian." When his daughter
throws clichés about the "fatherland" in his face,
Romulus answers, "The state always calls itself 'fatherland' when it is getting ready to slaughter people."[3]

By the end of the play Romulus has, after all,
come close to becoming a tragic hero; all that is needed
now is for the Germans to kill him. But that does not

happen; he is pensioned. If we think of conventional codes of honor, the ending is a blatant anomaly: he has sacrificed his people, but he himself enjoys a peaceful old age.

In the three years between the first performance of *Romulus* and that of *Die Ehe des Herrn Mississippi* (*The Marriage of Mr. Mississippi*), on March 26, 1952, in Munich, Dürrenmatt wrote his first two detective novels: *Der Richter und sein Henker* (*The Judge and His Hangman*) and *Der Verdacht* (*The Quarry*). His interests in dealing realistically with the present in these novels may have led Dürrenmatt to choose a similarly realistic material for the stage. There are at least three versions of *The Marriage of Mr. Mississippi*. The first is full of theological discussion. Übelohe exhibits— according to Mississippi—"the fiery sign of grace"; he is a second Christ who receives "the Judas kiss" from the state prosecutor. In the later versions Dürrenmatt's use of theology is more subtle, and his language is less solemn.

The play has several levels of action, but the actions are less important than the ideas that motivate these actions. The figures resemble the figures in a chess game; the player is Dürrenmatt, who cares little whether his figures come to life as dramatic characters. They exist so that he can put his thoughts into their mouths. Quite likely, Dürrenmatt did not have a clearly defined plot in the beginning. Bänziger has commented on the lack of design in the play: "Indeed, Dürrenmatt was obviously more the curious experimenter than the true creator in this macabre, grotesque work."[4]

From version to version the intentions grow clearer, and the results are more convincing. But only with the film version does Dürrenmatt succeed in giving the whole a cohesive order. The fragmentary quality and the multiple levels of meaning of the play—as embodied in the disparate characters: Anastasia, the three idealists, the politician—are accepted by the audience because it is now clear from the very beginning (when Saint-Claude, who is shot dead, does not fall down but keeps on talking) that the play is a grotesque comedy.

The influences on the play seem to be as varied as its actions and characters. One is reminded of Strindberg, Brecht, Wedekind, and even Shakespeare and Shaw. When Dürrenmatt was accused by Wedekind's widow of plagiarizing the two Lulu plays, he pointed out that the relationship of Mississippi and Anastasia resembled the psychological situation of Romeo and Juliet.

When Christian Jauslin remarks that Dürrenmatt's stage directions in this play are, in fact, conversations with the reader, one is reminded of Shaw, whose habit was to converse with his reader in his introductions to plays, acts, and scenes. Anastasia does not particularly resemble Shaw's women, whose ruthlessness and single-mindedness have the goal of bearing nearly perfect children. She does, however, embody much of Wedekind's Lulu, but Anastasia's sex appeal is a considerably less important issue: Mississippi marries her mainly to punish himself; furthermore, her first husband was unfaithful. Lulu never had to suffer such humiliations.

The central ideas of the play can best be understood from the film version, which was published in Germany in 1966 in a single volume along with the third stage version. Saint-Claude announces the play's subject near the beginning: "This is the story of three men who wanted to change the world because injustice and disorder had become rampant."[5] One of the three men is Florestan Mississippi, who even as a child read the

Bible conscientiously. He later studied at Oxford and became state prosecutor. His desire is to rescue the decadent world through judicial severity; he would force it to morality through fear, by reinstating the Mosaic laws. The second man, Frédéric René Saint-Claude, comes from the proletariat, as does Mississippi. Saint-Claude, however, read *Das Kapital*, went to Moscow, and has become a professional revolutionary. The communist world-revolution, he believes, will rescue all humanity. The third man, Count Bodo von Übelohe-Zabernsee, studied medicine and has tried to become the ideal Christian, by curing people and giving his wealth to the poor. He offers love instead of justice.

The play shows that none of the three idealists can accomplish anything in the present world. The world belongs to ruthless pragmatists, to the politicians who adhere to no theory but can adapt themselves quickly and arbitrarily to any set of circumstances. Even justice is not absolute but is subject to opportunism. The minister of justice amplifies this concept: "As minister of justice, I must determine whether or not justice is politically acceptable. In one instance, one must behead in the name of God; in another, one must be merciful in the name of the Devil. No state can avoid acting thus."[6] When Mississippi confesses to poisoning his wife, the state prosecutor says to him: "I am sorry, old man, in the interest of justice, I cannot have you arrested."[7] Mississippi, who wants to tell the truth, lands in an insane asylum. Saint-Claude is shot by his own henchmen. And Übelohe is reduced to a ragged beggar at the charity clinic he himself had founded. So ends this parable about the impossibility of changing the world. In his last speech Übelohe identifies himself with Don Quixote: both have fought windmills.

Played off against these three idealists is Anas-

tasia. She poisoned her husband for two reasons: she
wanted to avenge herself on him and his mistress (Mississippi's first wife), and she wanted to be able to marry
her lover, Count Übelohe. Übelohe had quite inno-
cently obtained poison tablets for her. When he found
out that she used them to kill her husband and not her
sick dog, he fled to Borneo. As the play opens, Anastasia must choose either to be executed as a murderess
or to marry Mississippi. She chooses the second. When it
is later to her advantage, she sleeps with Saint-Claude
also. She denies to Mississippi that she had ever loved
Übelohe, while the latter is standing beside her. She
finally ends up as the wife of the state president.

In every case Anastasia opts for life and comes
out each time on top—because she has no ideals. She
lies, murders, betrays, and adapts herself constantly;
this is her formula for getting along in the world. Although in the stage version she dies of poisoning, even
here Dürrenmatt shows how, with her final gasps, she
continues to lie.

The view of life as expressed in this play is just as
despairing as that in *Der Blinde*. The cynicism of the
later plays is anticipated: justice is for sale, as in *Der
Besuch der alten Dame* (*The Visit*); men of good will
can be found only in insane asylums, as in *Die Physiker*
(*The Physicists*); the woman wins in the brutal marital
war (*Play Strindberg*). Yet *The Marriage of Mr. Mississippi* does not seem morose, because it is comic in its
details. Dürrenmatt achieves the same effects as Chaplin, by using gags, paradoxical definitions, grotesque
actions, and parodies of Brecht and himself.

Chaplin's films *The Great Dictator* and *Modern
Times* present, as a whole, a tragic picture of the world.
The comic effect is a result of the details. Similarly,
after Saint-Claude is shot and Anastasia is poisoned,

neither is hindered from continued participation in the play. As in the Austrian dramatist Johann Nestroy's works, the characters do not break down when they have heard terrible news: they ask for a cup of coffee or a cognac. Anastasia, the revolutionaries, and the politicians are so maliciously exaggerated that the audience ultimately does not take them seriously on an emotional level; their arguments and actions are more amusing than enraging.

In an essay in the book *Der unbequeme Dürrenmatt* [The Incommodious Dürrenmatt], Fritz Buri reaches the conclusion that the coming of grace is a central motif in Dürrenmatt's dramas. This is especially true in the case of *Ein Engel kommt nach Babylon* (*An Angel Comes to Babylon*). The setting of Babylon has even more meaning than the unspecified European city in *The Marriage of Mr. Mississippi.* It symbolizes the Earth, an absurd little planet, a dot compared to the Andromeda Galaxy, home of the Angel who appears on Earth and brings with him the girl Kurrubi. The Angel resembles Voltaire's Micromégas, who, coming from another planet, observes the Earth from a perspective different from that of its inhabitants. This perspective enables him to recognize the absurdities of man's habits. In Dürrenmatt's drama, the Earthmen are fighting about political, social, and theological ideas, while the Angel travels around, observing and enjoying the magnificence of the planet. He knows the universe, but he had never seen anything more beautiful than nature on this tiny sphere. In nature, God gave man something splendid, a special favor, a blessing whose value men cannot even begin to comprehend.

Kurrubi as well as nature symbolizes heavenly grace. While the message of Kafka's emperor (in *The*

Castle) never gets through to men, grace in the form of Kurrubi is delivered in time to save them. But the result is the same: men remain without grace. Why? Because they want no part of it. Grace is set aside for him who is poorest, and it appears to Kurrubi that King Nebuchadnezzar, who is disguised as a beggar, is the poorest. For this reason, Kurrubi falls in love with him at first sight and wishes to be his companion.

Nebuchadnezzar, however, literally steps on grace (by throwing Kurrubi down and stepping on her). Although he wants to marry Kurrubi (to receive grace), he is not willing to give up his status as king (his earthly possessions). Kurrubi desires to give herself only to the most impoverished, but, in this wealthy land, no man is prepared to sacrifice his possessions for the sake of grace. Nebuchadnezzar resembles the youth whom Christ advised to give his wealth away. In the end Kurrubi (grace) forsakes Babylon (the world), since no one wanted her.

In the past the loss of God's grace would have been no theme for a comedy. In our present age, however, such a theme can only be presented under the mask of irony, parody, or satire; in short, it must be portrayed as a comedy. The author can only hope that a part of the public actually will perceive the core of bitterness behind the laughter.

One of the standard comic devices Dürrenmatt uses is mistaken identity. Nebuchadnezzar is disguised as a beggar and consistently loses out in his duel with the real beggar, Akki. Akki rescues everyone possible, finally even Kurrubi, by appearing in the mask of an executioner. Despite his comic cynicism, Akki is the only character who holds the audience's sympathy from beginning to end. On one hand, he is a thoroughgoing realist who takes advantage of others' prejudices and comes out of every situation on top: "Act dumb, and you'll live to grow old."[8] On the other hand, he is an idealist because, if he wanted, he could easily enough have a career and achieve power. He is the only person who fosters the arts, although he is well aware of the fact that 90 percent of his efforts is wasted on poets who have not a spark of talent.

Side by side with the sophisticated humor, there is a great deal of slapstick and local jokes. When Akki opens a sarcophagus, out jumps a poet; just about everybody picks up the guitar and spouts trite verses. Anyone from Switzerland will immediately smile to himself at the king's nickname, "Nebi," because it is identical with the short name of the national humor newspaper, *Nebelspalter* [Fog Splitter]. Also in the realm of low comedy is Akki's exchange of clothes with the hangman (one is reminded of the Torturer in *Die Stadt*).

Dürrenmatt often wittily questions his own underlying premise: What is the real reason God prefers people without possessions? When the Angel says, "The poorer a man is, the more pleasing he is to heaven," Nebuchadnezzar is astonished and asks, "Why is that?" The Angel considers the question but finds no answer. He, too, has prejudices that he has never examined. Finally, Dürrenmatt avenges himself on Tilly Wedekind for her accusations of plagiarism. At one point, Akki says: "Always the same old story. As soon as anybody starts to write creatively, he is accused of plagiarism."[9]

The Visit is Dürrenmatt's best play and the one that has least worried the author: since its first performance, on January 29, 1956, he has made only minor textual changes. Inasmuch as its locality is typi-

cally Swiss, this tragicomedy has indeed become a kind
of second national drama for Switzerland. While Schiller's *William Tell* depicts the awakening of a people to
freedom, *The Visit* demonstrates the spiritual and intellectual corruption of a community. Elisabeth Brock-
Sulzer stresses the importance of the play's focus: "The
concept of the community is central to Switzerland and
its identity. Whoever still has doubts about Dürrenmatt's immutably Swiss nature will think differently
after having read this work."[10] That the place and
character names, the arrangement of the railway station
with its separate rest rooms, and the habits of the
townspeople are typically Swiss—this cannot be
doubted. And the actions of the play question those
very traits which are said to characterize the Swiss:
honesty, foresight, thrift, skepticism, individualism.
Nonetheless, the incidents in *The Visit* remind one
more of the American mania for living on credit than of
the financial habits of a small Swiss town.

When the curtain goes up on the first act, the
audience sees the railway station of the city of Güllen.
Once the international European express trains stopped
here; now only local dayliners drop an occasional pas-
senger—usually a bailiff from the provincial capital trying to find something to confiscate. But there are not
many valuables left: the town and its individual citizens
are all bankrupt—an almost unbelievable phenomenon
in a world of thriving industrial development. While the
neighboring towns prosper, Güllen (the word means
"liquid manure") lives in poverty. The industries have
closed down, and everybody is on welfare.

Neither the citizens of Güllen nor the spectators
have the slightest idea why the town should be in such a
disastrous financial position. And at the moment nobody has time to think of possible answers because

Mrs. Claire Zachanassian is expected to arrive by train. She is the richest woman in the world. Seventy years ago she was born and raised in Güllen; everybody expects her to do something about the economic situation of her home town. Her one-time lover Alfred Ill has been asked by the townspeople to influence the rich woman discreetly.

The arrival of Mrs. Zachanassian is grotesque. She makes the express stop at Güllen by pulling the emergency brake. And she does not descend from the train alone: servants, reporters, two husbands, and a horde of other people accompany her; a caged panther and a beautiful coffin are carried across the stage. Neither the Gülleners nor the spectators have a clue about the purpose of these things, nor do they understand Mrs. Zachanassian's remarks. She tells the doctor that his next diagnosis should be a heart attack, and she asks the athlete whether he is strong enough to strangle a man. Only at the end of the first act do we learn what Mrs. Zachanassian wants: she wants justice and is willing to pay a hundred million francs for it, with half of the money to be distributed among the citizenry. Everybody would become rich. What does she mean by justice?

When she was a young girl, she was in love with Alfred Ill. When she expected a child by him, he produced two false witnesses who testified that they, too, had made love to Claire. Therefore, according to the law, it could not be established that Ill was the father of the child. He abandoned Claire to her fate and married a girl with money. From then on, Claire was considered a whore by everyone and had to leave Güllen. The child died. Now, half a century later, she asks for a correction of the former mistrial. This is not possible, according to the law. And there seems to be no need for such a correction: she has become a rich woman and has seen the world; she has been able to realize her every wish. Ill, on the other hand, has suffered, has remained poor, is married to a stupid woman, is the father of two children who do not love or respect him and who suffer from a lack of kindness.

No one intends to accept Mrs. Zachanassian's offer. They are not going to break the law and kill Ill. Many would have acted as he had, and everybody thinks that Ill has, meanwhile, been amply punished for his youthful tricks. But somehow they cannot resist the temptation to believe that, one way or another, they are going to get Claire's money in the end. Everybody begins buying on credit—even Ill's wife and children. Ill is horrified. The debts are growing. They have to be paid. After a while, the Gülleners convince themselves that Ill really must die after all. They suggest that he commit suicide. Their consciences seem to be adaptable to economic necessities: as their debts increase, their misgivings about Ill's former crime increase as well. In the end everybody (except the teacher) is convinced that Ill must die, not because of Claire's offer, of course, but because he did wrong half a century ago. Mrs. Zachanassian is quite right: justice must be done.

But has Claire set out to destroy only Alfred Ill? All her actions indicate that from the beginning she wanted to take her revenge on all the inhabitants of Güllen. She feels that she was driven away by *all* the townspeople. The town made her into a whore and now she is turning the townspeople into murderers. Her plan has genius: she punishes Ill through the townspeople and the townspeople through Ill.

In the third act we hear why Güllen has become a poor town: Claire bought up all industries and closed them down. Almost every building in Güllen belongs to her. Without her good will, Güllen has no chance ever to prosper again. With Ill dead, on the other hand, Güllen will at once become an industrial center again: the town officials will gain higher rank; the pastor will become a bishop; the teacher, a college professor. Ill must die. And, like a tragic hero, he begins to believe in his own guilt. Why has Claire become such a human devil? Because he rejected her when she was poor, exchanged her love for the money of another woman. Ill is responsible for the grotesque human being that Claire has become.

Although Dürrenmatt refuses to admit it, the "old lady" is more than Claire Zachanassian: she corresponds to the merciless God in Dürrenmatt's early works. The teacher says to Ill: "I know that an old lady will come to us, too, one day; and that the same thing will happen to us that is now happening to you. . . ."[11]

The Visit exposes the dubiousness of human logic: the Gülleners' reasoning is based solely on utilitarian values. Human conscience does not control man's actions; conscience is applied to those actions of man that are motivated by egoism. Such egoistical actions are subsequently designated as good by the conscience. The townspeople begin to despise and hate Ill so that they may then kill him with a "clean conscience." He becomes the scapegoat in the familiar ritual. From the audience's point of view, Ill's punishment has no real relation to his guilt because he has long since done penance through his miserable life. Ill's fate is an extension of the actions of the sadistic, revengeful God of Dürrenmatt's early works. But in *The Visit* Dürrenmatt has given, for the first time, a visible face to his evil God—that of Claire Zachanassian.

4

_Four
Detective
Stories
and
a Comic
Novel_

Dürrenmatt's four detective novels have attained the same international renown as his dramas; they are widely read in England and America as well as on the Continent. They are, to be sure, typically Dürrenmatt, but in no way do they depart from what one usually expects from a detective story. Dürrenmatt wrote the first two, *The Judge and His Hangman* and *The Quarry* in 1950 and 1951; they were published in serial form in the *Beobachter*. If he had not needed money at the time, Inspector Bärlach, protagonist of both novels, would never have been created.

The central subject of *The Judge and His Hangman* is the struggle between two people, one of whom is an idealistic detective. One character attempts—while preserving the appearance of legitimacy—to get rid of the other by staging a murder in such a way that all the circumstances will incriminate the other character. John Creasey's "Baron" novels often have this theme: the "Baron" works himself out of these traps by fighting against those who put him into the situation and also by making sure the police do not catch him before he himself has caught the real murderer. Similarly Erle Stanley Gardner's private eye, Donald Lam, is mainly occupied in extricating himself from "frames" by presenting the police with the guilty party.

For the most part, criminals set such traps for the "good detective"; rarely does one find the same plot in reverse, whereby the "good guy" is forced to employ criminal devices. In the case of an outstandingly intelligent criminal, against whom one could never prove anything otherwise, the reader is prepared to allow the good detective to eliminate the "bad guy" by framing him for a crime which he did not commit. Dashiell Hammett, Raymond Chandler, Rex Stout, and Georges Simenon all used this plot before Dürrenmatt.

The representative of good, Inspector Bärlach, has cancer and does not have much time left in which to bring the criminal to justice. The criminal Gastmann, because of his international connections, is so immune to police power that he cannot be touched through legal channels. Bärlach has Gastmann watched by a police officer. When the latter is murdered, the inspector seizes the opportunity to implicate Gastmann, who, to be sure, is not the murderer. Gastmann realizes that Bärlach plans to frame him, and, for the first time in their personal feud of twenty years, he gets frightened and prepares his escape.

But Bärlach is one step ahead of him: he knows the real murderer. The murderer has an obvious interest in Gastmann's conviction because it would divert suspicion from himself. He challenges Gastmann and emerges victor from their exchange of bullets. By turning him from a murderer into an executioner, Bärlach is able to mete out judgment on Gastmann. Of course, Bärlach's tactics are unfair, but under these circumstances the end seems to justify the means.

What sort of man is this Bärlach? His humanity reminds one of Georges Simenon's Inspector Maigret. Like him, Bärlach is of the old school, a man of strong character and a conservative. He does not think much of modern criminology and prefers to follow his own intuition, sharpened by experience and healthy common sense. Maigret is involved in constant battles with his superior, Coméliau, whose role Dürrenmatt assigns to the examining magistrate of Bern, Lutz. Both Lutz and Coméliau are pompous and conceited nitwits. The reader of Simenon's novels sees with Maigret's eyes and usually knows just as much as Maigret himself. On the contrary, Bärlach, in the first novel, knows more than the reader; the reader is shocked by the conclusion.

Bärlach is a government employee and is, by nature of his profession, obligated to eliminate lawbreakers. His instinct for justice seems, however, to be more deeply-rooted, although he believes in neither God nor life after death. In this respect, Bärlach is reminiscent of Mike Shayne, Pete MacGrath, Travis McGee, and their like. The prototype of this outwardly stone-hard, inwardly existentialist-nihilistic detective was created in the twenties and thirties by Hammett. The best-known examples are Chandler's Philip Marlow and Ross MacDonald's Lew Archer.

These detectives have no ties. They have neither relatives nor friends; usually, they are divorced. Love is an empty word for them. Money interests them only inasmuch as it provides them with their daily ration of alcohol and cigarettes. They waste no thoughts on God. They are endowed, in the same way as Hemingway's hard-boiled adventurers, with a certain sympathy for the socially disadvantaged. They are skeptics who have seen through the lies of today's world. Like members of Kamikaze troops, they venture into the greatest dangers, from which they seldom emerge unscathed.

Why, then, their fanatic fight against murder? With them it acts as a substitute for religion. Bärlach resembles these men in many ways. For him, too, women, love, relatives, country, and God are of little importance. But he continues to fight crime to the bitter end—even on his deathbed. Bärlach's pleasures, too, are limited: they consist of eating, drinking, and smoking.

Although *The Judge and His Hangman* stands in the best tradition of American and French detective stories, Elisabeth Brock-Sulzer is justified in saying that the novel is, in part, a parody (see, for example the ridiculous actions of the village policeman when he finds the corpse) and that Dürrenmatt has used it as a vehicle for autobiographical material. The action takes place in the area around Ligerz, where Dürrenmatt lived when he wrote it. Inhabitants of his native region, the Emmenthal, appear in both novels. In *The Judge* Gastmann's two maliciously stupid servants are Emmenthalers; in *The Quarry* the Emmenthaler is the bigoted and hopelessly dumb nurse, Kläri. It is no coincidence that the depraved doctor in the latter novel is called Emmenberger.

Dürrenmatt must have had great fun in writing these novels. It is much easier to insert incidental material in a novel than in a play. In the first half of *The Judge,* there is not a page without its touch of humor. Dürrenmatt ridicules the police, the people of Bern, the separatists from the Jura Mountains, state officials and their titles, the militarists, Swiss artists, and others. He administers such a heavy dose of symbolism that it becomes parody. ("Charon" is the name of the car that carries first Schmied, then Tschanz to their deaths. After Schmied's death, Bärlach no longer eats in the restaurant "Schmiedstube," but rather in the "Du Théâtre.") Dürrenmatt's irony climaxes in the chapter in which the omniscient authorial narrator lets himself be interrogated by Bärlach and Tschanz. It turns out that both the inspector and the narrator are great enthusiasts of fine cooking and that they share the same opinion about Gastmann. The aim of both their professions is to get at the heart of the matter. The narrator is the only person other than Bärlach who has seen through Gastmann.

The Quarry offers no less suspense than *The Judge and His Hangman*. Here, however, the issue is not discovering the murderer but rather finding out how Bärlach gets out of the trap in which he has let himself be caught. Bärlach has come through an operation, and one assumes that he will live only one more year. He is lying in the Hospital Salem in Bern (in which Dürrenmatt's father was chaplain) and is, symbolically, reading *Life* magazine.

A photograph in *Life* arouses the suspicions of Bärlach's doctor; the doctor wonders whether the infamous Doctor Nehle, who operated without anesthesia in the Stutthof concentration camp, might not be identical with Dr. Emmenberger, the head of a private clinic in Zurich. Bärlach should, by rights, have every reason to let someone else handle this particular case. In the first place, he has just retired; in the second, he ought to have the right to enjoy his last year of life in peace. He is driven not by moral obligation but rather by intractable spite, the determination "to see things through in this world and to fight for something else, something better than just to struggle with this tortured body of his, racked with cancer. . . ."[1]

What the inspector undertakes is insane, but in the best tradition of the tough private eyes who enter the lion's den with clenched fists and little consideration of the risks involved. Bärlach has himself transferred incognito to Emmenberger's clinic. Only the journalist Fortschig and Doctor Hungertobel are aware of his secret. If Emmenberger should find out the truth about his "false" patient, he would have to kill only three people to remain undiscovered. Bärlach neglects the standard trick of leaving behind a sealed envelope which, if he were to disappear, would be handed over to the police on a certain date. He could also have set up a daily telephone conversation with someone, who, if Bärlach did not answer, would immediately have notified the police.

But the inspector falls blindly into the trap. On the day of his retirement, newspapers print his picture; thus, Emmenberger knows who his patient is. Fortschig publishes an article that no one takes seriously, and from that point, the situation cannot be reversed. The journalist dies, supposedly of a heart attack, and Bärlach finds himself in a prison-like operating room. Hungertobel's murder is already planned, and Emmenberger's chances of escape are almost guaranteed. From here, the plot progresses as in Edgar Allan Poe's "The Pit and the Pendulum": Bärlach watches the hands of a clock one whole night long, because at 7 a.m. he is to be operated on—without anesthesia; in other words, he is to be killed. During this emotional tension, there is also a great deal of meditation on life and death; good and evil; faith, God, and justice.

Of primary significance to Dürrenmatt is an analysis of the nihilist and existentialist Emmenberger. One can compare him to the sadistic God of the early works. This doctor enjoys torturing others; it gives him a sense of power. The Jew who rescues Bärlach in the end places men in two categories: the tormentors and the tormented. Emmenberger is clearly a tormentor. Dr. Edith Marlok, whom Emmenberger has chained to himself through drug addiction, calls her own lover a "torturer." She is in a position to avenge herself on him but does not: "Our precept that the fight against evil must never under any circumstances be abandoned is valid only in a vacuum or only on paper, but not on this planet, on which we rush through the cosmos like witches on a broom."[2]

Bärlach's conversations with Edith Marlok and Emmenberger form the high point of the novel. Both doctors think, in the truest sense of the word, Dürrenmatt's thoughts. They think and act completely consist-

ently—with horrifying results. Dürrenmatt rejects their
actions, but he respects the philosophy that motivates
those actions. Bärlach, like Dürrenmatt, has nothing
with which to oppose this philosophy—no faith. All
that remains for him, if he is honest with himself, is
silence. Or else he can, with the Jew, cry out, "Long
live mankind!" and add, "But how?" The enigma of
existence is man's fate:

There we are, without being asked, set on some crumbling
shoal or other, without knowing why. Here we are, staring
into a universe, monstrous in its emptiness and monstrous
in its fullness, a senseless waste. And here we are pushing
on toward distant cataracts, which we are bound to reach
sometime. This is all we know. Thus we live in order to
die; thus we breathe and speak; thus we love; and thus we
bear children and the children of children, only to be
turned into carrion with those whom we love and whom
we have brought forth out of our flesh, only to fall victim
to the indifferent, nonliving elements out of which we were
made.[3]

This is not Edith Marlok speaking; it is Dürrenmatt.

Again and again, Dürrenmatt has said that he is
not a nihilist. Emmenberger, too, resents being called a
nihilist:

Everything that one undertakes, the positive deed as well as
the negative, depends on luck. Evil and good fall into one's
lap as in a game of chance; chance justifies and chance
condemns. But everyone who senses a threat to himself
always has at his disposal the big word "nihilist," which he
throws with grandiose manner and even greater conviction
into the face of him who threatens.[4]

Thereupon Emmenberger sets forth his credo. He
believes, first of all, in material things. Second, he believes in himself: "I *am*—as a part of this matter, atom,

strength, mass, molecule—just like you, and . . . my existence gives me the right to do whatever I want to." Nothing has significance; everything can be exchanged; "it is immaterial whether things are or are not." Since matter cannot be just, there is no justice. Bärlach sums it up: "You believe in nothing except in the right to torture men!"[5]

Emmenberger admits as much. Torturing creates in him the feeling that he momentarily controls matter; this may be the reason why God is a sadist. Although Bärlach professes nothing that can stand in sharp contrast to the doctor's confession, Bärlach is different, perhaps by accident. Like the Jew, he has the ability to imagine himself in the position of the tormented. He can feel compassion, and, as a result, he wishes to punish the tormentor. Bärlach is no longer physically capable of doing anything; but the Jew—formerly among the tormented, now an avenger—carries out the punishment. Bärlach returns to Bern. To what end? To let himself be consumed alive for one more year by cancer.

Dürrenmatt's third detective novel, *Das Versprechen (The Pledge)*, originated in 1958 together with the script for the film version, *Es geschah am hellichten Tag* [It Happened in Broad Daylight], which he had written on contract to the producer Lazar Wechsler for Praesens Film. The peddler von Gunten finds the mutilated body of the girl Gritli Moser in the woods. Commissioner Matthäi promises the parents to catch the murderer. With the exception of Matthäi, everyone thinks that the peddler, who has a record, is guilty. He is interrogated for so long that, in despair, he hangs himself in his cell. This seems to prove his guilt.

Matthäi, however, is not satisfied. Similar crimes

had happened two and five years before, both on the road between Zurich and Chur. The commissioner concludes that the murderer must be a traveling salesman, a psychopath who drives a car. He lays a trap for him: he takes over a gas station and invites a woman with a child (who resembles Gritli Moser), to live with him. Their house lies on the road from Chur to Zurich.

In the film, Matthäi's plot is successful: he catches the murderer. In the novel (whose subtitle reads, significantly, "Requiem on the Detective Novel"), the commissioner fails. The murderer, on his way to the place where he plans to meet the child and where Matthäi and the police are waiting, is killed in a car accident. Chance has spoiled the commissioner's logical plans. His colleagues don't take him seriously any more. Stubbornly he keeps waiting for years; he begins to drink, and he degenerates. Many years later, a dying woman admits that her mentally disturbed husband had had the three murders on his conscience and had planned the fourth; because of the fatal accident, he had not been able to go through with it.

Dürrenmatt's narrative technique in *The Pledge* is considerably more mature than in his first two novels. He chooses Matthäi's former superior as narrator; the story is being told to Dürrenmatt. Whereas his earlier dialogues were often too long and complicated to be believed as actual conversation, Dürrenmatt now exercises greater discipline and goes so far as to apologize to the reader for changing a word or so of the narrator's account. The criminologist-narrator could be Bärlach; the two men have a similar understanding of criminal cases. Matthäi's boss knows that crime often does pay, and he relates his subordinate's story in order to prove what Gastmann in *The Judge* had always known: a crime can happen through chance, and it can be solved

—or not solved—through chance as well. As the narrator says: "Reality can be got at only partly through logic."[6]

As in the first novel, autobiographical and humorous elements play an important role. Dürrenmatt lets the narrator suddenly turn into a critic of Dürrenmatt: "I am really getting angry about the plots of your novels."[7] Dürrenmatt does not hesitate to bring up repeatedly the same themes, the same situations, the same aspects of his concept of life. The scene in front of the Mägenwil Inn reminds one of *The Visit.* The people erroneously believe that the peddler is the murderer. They threaten the detective-inspector and are ready to lynch the peddler on the spot. The inspector makes an unexpected move. He tells the people that he and the policemen will "hand over the peddler to you as soon as we are convinced that you want justice."[8] The people do want justice, of course, but, unlike *The Visit*, there is no money involved, and so they finally leave the peddler to the police.

There are references to other Dürrenmatt works as well. The narrator, for example, rides on the same train from Bern to Zurich that had disappeared (1952) in "Der Tunnel." The insane asylum, in which Matthäi seeks out the psychiatrist, recalls *The Physicists.* Once again, through the doctor, Dürrenmatt expresses his opinion of what man is: "The will, with which men must combat their impulses, is abnormally weak; it takes damned little—irregular metabolism, a few degenerated cells—to make man an animal."[9]

Die Panne (*Traps*, 1956), exists in two versions—as a short novel and as a radio play. Although written before *The Pledge, Traps* stands apart from the other three novels in that it is not properly a detective novel.

It is nonetheless connected to them by illustrating the
following passage from *The Quarry*:

There are any number of crimes that people ignore only
because they are somewhat more aesthetic than a murder,
which slaps you right in the face and gets into the newspapers to boot. Both kinds of crime, however, amount to
the same thing—if you look at them closely and use your
imagination. Imagination, that's the key, imagination!
Often, with a total lack of imagination, a worthy business-
man commits a crime between his apéritif and lunch
by doing a bit of underhanded business, but no one
pays any attention to it at all, especially the business-
man himself, because no one possesses the imagination to
see it.[10]

Traps is this kind of an unimaginative character
who shares the guilt for the death of his boss without
being aware of it. The grotesque trial in the novel
makes Traps conscious of his guilt. In the radio version
he has already, by the next day, forgotten what he does
not want to know and is priming himself for his next
crime; in the novel, he executes justice on himself.

Many things in *Traps* remind one of Kafka's *The
Trial*; this is especially true of the narrative version. In
Kafka's novel the trial and K.'s guilt remain mysteri-
ous; perhaps they have to be interpreted theologically.
In Dürrenmatt's work, however, Traps is unquestiona-
bly guilty, although the court remains grotesque
enough. The introductory chapter is not directly narrative; it is a meditation about the role of a writer in the
modern world. What is there left for an author to write
about, if he does not want to write about his ego, if fate
has withdrawn into the background because of over-
planning, if, because of the H-bomb and the computer,
the destruction of our planet through mechanical failure
can occur at any moment? No longer do "a God, jus-

tice, or fate" threaten, but rather accidents such as the "explosion of a nuclear power plant, brought on by a negligent lab technician."[11] These reflections are connected with the tale inasmuch as they make ironic and ludicrous Traps's exposure and guilt.

Grieche sucht Griechin (*Once A Greek*, 1955) is a comic novel that resembles in spirit *Frank der Fünfte*. Dürrenmatt calls the novel a "prose comedy." As in Twain, much of the humor is a result of the grotesque exaggerations. Swiss readers will recognize wordplays in names of persons, firms, and places. The Swiss-naturalized Greek, Archilochos, is a petit bourgeois par excellence, a bureaucrat. He is set in his ways, fat, ugly, and stupid. Probably the only reason he is made to be a Greek is that his proper name (Arschloch—"ass hole") can thus be playfully disguised.

Through his newspaper advertisement seeking a marriage partner, he meets the leading courtesan of the city, a paragon of beauty, wealth, and good nature, the angelic Chloé, who wants to retire from her profession into a family life—with the blessings of her clientele, who think her retirement well-deserved. Her grateful patrons (from the prime minister and the bishop to the industrial tycoon Petit-Paysan) promote the welfare of Chloé's fiancé without reservation: the dunce becomes a Director-General of a large industrial firm and a head of the World Church. Finally he notices what sort of a past his fiancée has had and runs away—horrified. But not forever: in a special "conclusion for lending libraries" everything turns out right.

One could, of course, interpret Chloé as the "grace" granted to Archilochos. In this case, she would be a second Kurrubi (*An Angel Comes to Babylon*). And there are occasional paragraphs that support this

comparison, such as this speech of the prime minister
to Archilochos:

You have been given grace . . . there are two possible
reasons for grace coming to you, and it depends on you
which one applies: one is love, if you believe in love, and
the other is evil, if you do not believe in love. Love is a
miracle that can happen again and again; evil is a fact that
is always at hand. Justice damns evil, hope wants to make
things better, and love forgives. Only love can accept grace
as it is. There is nothing more difficult, I know. The world
is terrible and senseless. The hope that some sense lies
behind all the nonsense, behind all the terror, can be pre-
served only by those who love in spite of everything.[12]

This speech is one of the few passages about love in all
of Dürrenmatt's works.

    Grieche sucht Griechin is a crazy, bold, hair-rais-
ing comedy, a satirical fairy tale about boom times.
German literature can offer little as enjoyable as this
funny and grotesque novel.

5

*Radio
Plays*

A volume of Dürrenmatt's collected radio plays, published in 1962, contains eight titles. Of these, "Die Panne" has already been discussed; "Herkules und der Stall des Augias" [Hercules and the Augean Stables, 1954] was expanded into a stage play in 1963 and will be treated in the next chapter. The remaining plays are "Der Doppelgänger" [The Double, written in 1946, published in 1960], "Der Prozess um des Esels Schatten" [The Lawsuit About the Donkey's Shadow, 1951], "Nächtliches Gespräch mit einem verachteten Menschen" [Nocturnal Conversation with a Despised Man, 1952], "Stranitzky und der Nationalheld" [Stranitzky and the National Hero, 1952], "Das Unternehmen der Wega" [Operation Wega, 1955], and "Abendstunde im Spätherbst" ("Incident at Twilight," 1957).

Dürrenmatt wrote his radio plays during the period when earning money was still very important to him. That they are outstanding examples of their genre is, however, not open to doubt. Dürrenmatt has won some of the most highly respected awards for radio plays: in 1956, the Prize of the War Blind for "Die Panne"; and in 1958, the Prix d'Italia for "Incident at Twilight."

Thematically, "Der Doppelgänger" belongs to the world of *Die Stadt* and the early dramas. A man finds himself suddenly face to face with his double. The double has killed someone, and the court wishes the man to take the guilt upon himself. Like Kafka's K. in *The Trial*, the man is not acquainted with the court, nor can he comprehend why he should let himself be punished for something he did not do. The double argues with strange logic: "You would have acted as I did, had you been tempted as I was tempted. My guilt is your guilt. Our faces are alike, as are our bodies, our souls, and the very roots of our being."[1] At first the man remains unconvinced and swears that he would never kill a fellow human being.

Dürrenmatt concerns himself with two subjects here: the idea of the Christian God, and the condition of a man who faces God and his incomprehensible justice. The man is led into temptation; in spite of his best intentions, he kills and must assume guilt. His mistake seems to have been that he refused to take his double's guilt upon himself. Had he done so, he would have been "free," says the double.

The man, his double, and the producer exhibit three different patterns of thinking. (1) The double thinks like Dürrenmatt's God: since every man is guilty (sins of the fathers), he should humbly accept any punishment to which the court (God) sentences him. God does not concern himself with people anyway: he is too great for that. If anyone has committed a crime, someone must do penance for it. Who this sufferer is appears to be a matter of indifference to God. (2) The producer thinks like a down-to-earth realist: "No one can be condemned for an offence he did not commit."[2] The strange court stirs him to indignation, and he proceeds to the little castle (compare with Kafka's *The Castle*) where the judges supposedly hold court. Symbolically, he finds no one there; in reality (or at least for realists) there is no God. (3) At first the man thinks like a realist, but then he is persuaded to accept his guilt: "I was a murderer without having killed; I was guilty of a death, without having committed a crime." The producer finds this thinking incomprehensible from a human point of view. The man says, "I have given up the human viewpoint." The logic of Christian theology, which seems enigmatic and paradoxical to the realist, is affirmed by the man: "There is nothing more beautiful than to surrender oneself to him [to the high court, God]. Only he who accepts injustice will find justice, and only he who succumbs will find mercy."[3]

Elisabeth Brock-Sulzer believes that in "Der Doppelgänger" Dürrenmatt is proclaiming Christian teaching: "Before God, we are all sinners." On the contrary, Dürrenmatt depicts the absurdity of such a principle, which contradicts all logic and any reasonable sense of justice. When the producer and the author find the castle empty, the former is enraged: "And I [as a man of reason] am to be satisfied with this?" The writer replies, "We *have* to be satisfied with it."[4]

On September 14, 1951, Dürrenmatt, having seen a performance of Schiller's *The Robbers*, wrote an article, stating that both Kleist's Kohlhaas (in *Michael Kohlhaas*) and Schiller's Kosinksy (in *The Robbers*) were right. But, he continued:

For the very reason that they are right, they are not free. And they would regain their freedom only by relinquishing their right to act. To relinquish one's rights means to bear injustice. That is, however, possible only where right is on God's side. This is Christian freedom: one need only be justified before God, or one can choose to bear an injustice. Before God, one is justified only by grace; and that is Abel. These are the Christian connections between grace and freedom.[5]

If, however, no God sits in the "castle," such convictions are untenable. And even if a god should be sitting there, his sort of right would continue to puzzle men. "Der Doppelgänger" is not a Christian play but rather an attempt to point out the absurdity of Christian thinking.

"Nächtliches Gespräch mit einem verachteten Menschen" is subtitled "A Course for Contemporaries." Only two voices are heard: that of the man and that of the "other one," the executioner, who climbs in through the window of the man's room. This man has been expecting the executioner, whom he contemptuously addresses in the familiar *du* form. The basic issue in this play is the art of dying, the acceptance of death as something unavoidable. Man has been condemned to die. All men know that one day the executioner (death) will come, but not all face the execution (dying) with equal aplomb.

The "other one's" task is to bring about the death of every type of man. Some men die proudly, speaking eloquently "of freedom and justice" and mocking "the powers that be" (God). The humble die best, the executioner claims, those persons who have willingly foresworn justice, innocent ones "about whom I well knew that my fatal blow was unjustly ordered."[6]

At first sight, an executioner who strikes down people whose innocence he knows seems despicable. But he is not concerned about justice in individual cases; he has realized that the only justice is that which "contradicts all reason": "If someone in the hour of his unjust death lays aside pride, fear, and indeed even his rights so that he dies as children die, without cursing the world, this man achieves a victory greater than any victory ever gained by a mighty one."[7] The man permits himself to be converted and says to Death: "But when things have gone so far that you, with your monstrous form, climb down out of the empty heavens and into our rooms, then we may become humble again. Then we are faced with something which is not self-evident—with the forgiveness of our sins, with peace for our souls."[8]

What is the meaning of the play? Dürrenmatt has attempted to observe the human situation through the

eyes of neither God nor man, but through those of
God's death figure. The heavens are as empty as the
little castle in "Der Doppelgänger." God does not exist,
or at least he does not let anyone find him. If he did
exist, then the individual man—an ant crawling around
on the earth—would be completely unimportant to him.
The idea that God owes justice to anybody is absurd. It
would be just as absurd if we were to establish a law for
ants which ran contrary to their natural instincts, and if
we were then to call each ant to account for individual
infractions of this law. We human beings are best off
being humble; our best solution is to accept our ridiculous situation, to give up any idea of our own importance, and to embrace death as a matter of course.

The inhabitants of Venus in "Das Unternehmen
der Wega" have found this happy relationship with
death. Death brings both forgiveness for sins and peace
of mind: "The rest does not matter to us." Certainly, it
does not matter to God, who is not even sitting on his
throne. In contrast to Eastern philosophers, Dürrenmatt does not mean that we should abandon the fight
for a better world. We can fight as much as we please.
The struggle is honorable, even if it is fundamentally
senseless.

The next group of radio plays falls in the same
period as the detective stories and the dramas after
Romulus. If the content seems just as somber as before,
it is nevertheless served up with humor—often grim
humor. The model for "Der Prozess um des Esels
Schatten" was the fourth part of Christoph Martin Wieland's novel *Geschichte der Abderiten* [History of the
Abderites, 1773], from which Dürrenmatt took the
story of the trial between the donkey driver Anthrax
and the dentist Struthion.

Dürrenmatt adds to his title, "according to Wieland—but not all that much." If one has not read the

novel, he will miss certain allusions. Dürrenmatt is usually more drastic than Wieland. In Wieland's work the chambermaid refuses to stand up for the donkey driver, and Anthrax has to give his daughter Gorgo to the priest (as a mistress) in order to get the latter's help. In Dürrenmatt, Gorgo has to be sold as a slave so that Anthrax can pay his lawyer. In Wieland there was no question of a contrast of capitalists and proletariat. Dürrenmatt, however, makes full use of political and economic actualities; he introduces tourist unions and unions for the protection of animals, the workers' party, and munitions manufacturers. Wieland's novel has a happy ending, except for the poor donkey, who is torn to pieces by the populace. In Dürrenmatt's play Abdera is destroyed. Each faction sets fire to the opposition's temple, and since each fireman refuses to put out the fire in his opponent's temple, the whole city burns down.

In "Stranitzky" and "Herkules" the unmasking of national heroes is the main topic. Stranitzky and Anton are crippled war veterans. Stranitzky had been a soccer player but has lost his legs; Anton is strong as a bear, but blind. He carries Stranitzky around on his shoulders or pushes him in a cart; blind Anton is guided by Stranitzky. The two maimed men live in terrible poverty, alleviated only by Maria's love for Stranitzky. He, however, denies himself this love. He lives in the illusory hope that he, Anton, and the national hero Baldur von Moeve (who has a leprous toe and is surrounded by indulgent princesses) will found a new government to replace the one that has used the three of them as cannon fodder.

The present government distracts the people's concern from the true misery of the war-wounded by absorbing them in publicity about Moeve's toe. The dull-witted people are mocked for letting themselves be

deceived by the mass media; they have become totally
incapable of independent thinking. But even the poor
cripples have their Chaplinesque comic aspects. Stranitzky exaggerates whenever he recounts his soccer
days; cruel plays are made on his name (Stanislawsky,
Strapitzky).

Not a good word is said about the journalists and
the reporters. Even the radio station that broadcasts
Dürrenmatt's play is made fun of: Stranitzky's speech
for Radio Beromünster's (German Switzerland) program "Echo der Zeit" [Echo of the Times] is sup-
pressed because it is politically unsuitable. But Dürrenmatt is less concerned with social conditions than
with the destructive influences of the mass media on a
people that is growing rapidly more and more dumb; a
public that lets itself be taken in by a charlatan like
Moeve is bound to believe any drivel the media offer
them.

"Das Unternehmen der Wega" demonstrates the
ruthlessness of the modern state. The play takes place
in the year 2255, at a time in which a new world war
has become inevitable. The radio announcer speaks:
"Diplomacy has stretched its skills to the utmost. The
Cold War can no longer be drawn out. Peace is an
impossibility. The necessity of conducting a war is
greater than the fear of it."[9] Europe and America oppose Russia, Asia, and Australia. The half of the moon
that is strategically most valuable belongs to the Russians; therefore, the West decides to convince Venus to
join forces with it.

Venus (love) is a penal colony, a place of ban-
ishment; criminals and political undesirables from both
superstates on Earth have been regularly deported there
for two centuries. The climate is awful—hot and
humid. The surface undulates constantly so that one
can live only on ships. People are subjected to terrifying

dangers: diseases, monstrous animals, storms, sudden volcanic eruptions. The West hopes, with the help of the inhabitants, to set up weapons against the Eastern powers under the cover of Venus's hazy atmosphere.

What the delegation finds on the planet is not at all what they expected. The inhabitants have not formed a government. They have had no time for that; their sole occupation is survival. Every day the delegation has to deal with a different person—with whomever has time at the moment—because the others are out trying to find food. The residents of Venus are not prepared to take part in any sort of war. They are unmoved by the promise that they can come back to Earth after the victory. In Venus life is dangerous, to be sure, but it is honorable. People help one another; survival is their common purpose. Existence on Earth tempts not one inhabitant of Venus.

Life on Venus is considered a blessing because it is a rarity. Death seems natural and necessary, and for that reason dying is easy to accept. The delegation turns back without having achieved its goal, but not without having accomplished something at least. After their takeoff they bomb the planet and probably wipe out most of the inhabitants. This is done as a preventive measure against possible intervention by the Russians on Venus. This ending is typical of the sardonic humor of the play, which emphasizes its bleak seriousness.

"Incident at Twilight" is a brilliant satire on the writing profession, on Dürrenmatt himself, and above all on biographical criticism. Dürrenmatt purposely puts details of himself in the character of the writer, Maximilian Frederick Korbes (Herr Korbes "must have been an evil man," goes the Grimms' fairy tale). Korbes sits at his desk, describes both his room, with its view of the lake, and his own physical appearance.

Like Korbes, Dürrenmatt often mentions Don Quixote in his works. Some critics consider Dürrenmatt an "evil" man, one who tries to criticize everything. Herr Korbes is a real devil of a man, and he keeps a theologian as his secretary. Korbes has written more than twenty detective novels and has won a Nobel Prize for them.

A visitor, Feargod Hofer, comes into his suite. This visitor is a representative of biographical criticism. He has found out that Korbes himself has committed twenty-one of the twenty-two murders he describes in his novels.

Korbes is amused: "I have been interpreted in the light of psychology, Catholicism, Protestantism, existentialism, Buddhism, and Marxism, but never before in the way you have gone about it."[10] Later he admits, "I am only able to write about experiences I have had myself, because I lack fantasy."[11] Dürrenmatt means these words ironically about himself; for Korbes, they are true. If a critic is to be consistent in his exclusively biographical interpretation of an author, then he would logically have to conclude—in the case of an author who writes murder mysteries—that the author must have committed the murders himself. If not, how could he possibly provide the reader with solutions to the cases?

Biographical interpretation is relatively fruitless when applied to Dürrenmatt, who, by the way, despises the method. In the instance of Herr Korbes, however, the critic—absurdly enough—hits the nail on the head. With the greatest of pleasure Dürrenmatt takes his revenge on invaders of the privacy of the artist. Korbes throws the visitor out the window; the death is called a suicide. Korbes immediately uses the episode as the subject for a new radio play.

6

The Absurdity of Human Behavior

Two of Dürrenmatt's dramas were unsuccessful: *Frank der Fünfte* [Frank V] and the stage version of *Herkules und der Stall des Augias*. Initially, the subtitle of *Frank der Fünfte* read, "Opera About a Private Bank." Paul Burkhard wrote the music. He had previously composed, with Walter Lesch, *Die kleine Niederdorf-Oper* [Little Opera About Niederdorf],* a musical play that Dürrenmatt had highly praised in *Weltwoche*, January 11, 1952. It is clear that Dürrenmatt (like Brecht and Georg Kaiser before him) was taken by the idea of attempting a play with musical interludes. From the first performance on, Dürrenmatt's opera was called a weak imitation of Brecht's *The Threepenny Opera*. His self-justifications were to no avail: Dürrenmatt was unable to make the critics reconsider their verdict.

Even extensive textual revisions did little to redeem the failure; the text, printed in 1960, is a reworking of the 1959 Zurich stage script. In 1964 Dürrenmatt revised the play a second time; he made the stage directions more extensive and exact, took out several songs, rearranged one scene and changed the ending. Now the subtitle read, "A Comedy, with Music by Paul Burkhard." This third version was to have been presented in Bochum. After four weeks of rehearsals, Dürrenmatt had a falling out with the director and withdrew his play. Volume II of his collected plays (in German) contains the text of the Bochum version; the most recent edition of *Frank der Fünfte* includes both the final scenes of the 1959 Zurich version and of the published edition of 1960.

In an interview with Horst Bienek, Dürrenmatt said that he hit upon the theme of *Frank der Fünfte*

* Niederdorf is Zurich's bar and cabaret district.

72

after he had seen an English production of *Titus Andronicus* (directed by Peter Brook) in Paris, in 1958. This work of Shakespeare's youth struck Dürrenmatt as a "drama of atrocity," and Dürrenmatt felt he should write a similar play for the contemporary stage—"to incite children against their parents, to show a lover who has to murder his beloved. . . ."[1] Both these motifs appear in *Frank der Fünfte*, and Dürrenmatt has made clear his debt to Shakespeare: "*Frank der Fünfte* is modeled on a Shakespearean tragedy of royalty. I want to show a society similar to Shakespeare's, but described in contemporary terms. Therefore—and this is important—I must introduce a power structure other than the monarchy."[2] For his power structure Dürrenmatt chose a bank. Instead of kings, there are bank directors; instead of vassals and courtiers, there are clerks, cashiers, and personnel directors.

Like the Elizabethan drama's kings, these bank directors are, in fact, gangsters. They make their livings from crime. In *Frank der Fünfte* the special power struggle concerns a fifth-generation bank director who has become a humane weakling; he reads Goethe and Mörike and wants to liquidate the bank. However, his son, Frank VI, prevents his father from doing so by shoving him into the safe and taking over the direction of the bank. He has the gift to adapt himself to new circumstances; he becomes "the arch scoundrel needed in our times—respectable, hard, and evil."[3]

To praise a scoundrel in heroic tones is a comic device that Henry Fielding used in his novel *Jonathan Wild*. The reader knows at all times what Fielding is getting at. He does not consider the author perverse, stupid, or cynical; rather, he recognizes him as a brilliant parodist. It is the same with John Gay. With Brecht, however, there is a difference; unlike Dürrenmatt, Brecht believes that only the Western world has gone to the dogs. The characters of *The Threepenny Opera* demonstrate specifically the evils of capitalism. One thing detracts from their social effectiveness, however: these characters have become too sympathetic in the eyes of the theatergoer, and the conscience of Western audiences does not feel the slightest pangs when it sees the play.

Dürrenmatt's scoundrels are real scoundrels; but the spectator pities them (Egli, Böckmann, even Frank and Ottilie), and the whole set of circumstances is so improbable that the audience is irritated. Not even the main character is convincing: either Frank V longs to be good and gives up being a gangster boss, or it is as Dürrenmatt claims in the text for the Bochum program: "That Frank the Fifth does not despair is plain proof of his crime. If he were really possessed by the good spirit, as he claims, he could no longer live as a lawbreaker. But he is still able to break laws; this is why he is a blasphemer."[4] Dürrenmatt presents no logical arguments to support the idea that Frank V is too humane to continue as a gangster boss.

In his speech to the Munich critics (1963), Dürrenmatt stressed that Shakespeare was his model, not Brecht; that the play is about freedom, not justice; that the failure of the bank is a metaphor for the failure of democracy (if each man has a key to the safe, the state grows powerless); that "the unrestricted freedom of everybody becomes a threat to the human community."[5] All this may be true, but Dürrenmatt had to say it in a speech because the play says nothing of this sort.

In his essay "Theaterprobleme" ("Problems of the Theatre") Dürrenmatt claims that Brecht's dramas sometimes express the exact opposite of "that which they claim to express."[6] In the case of *Frank der Fünfte*, either the play does not express what Dürrenmatt wants to say, or the public and the critics are just too stupid to understand what Dürrenmatt means. Where is the problem? Like Dürrenmatt, we believe that the world has gone to the dogs. We find his creations credible: the awful doctor in *The Physicists*, who is going to destroy the world; the monstrous Wood of "Das Unternehmen der Wega," who wipes out the inhabitants of an entire planet; even the fall of Güllen's citizenry. But we cannot believe in the characters of *Frank der Fünfte*.

That Herbert becomes a scoundrel in Oxford and Franziska a whore in a Montreux boarding school—these actions are neither believable nor comical; they are just exaggerations. If Frank intends to liquidate the bank, why, then, does he go and hire Neukomm? How does such an absolutist national president fit into a democracy? How do Herbert and Franziska ever get together? Where do they get the money for the trip? Why are the parents not told that Franziska has left her boarding school? If Egli and Frieda do not marry, this is neither tragic nor comic: it is simply stupid of them (who otherwise are not dumb at all!).

Few figures in the play act logically or consistently; few act in keeping with their character, intelligence, or past histories. In the theater of the absurd people do not do that either, but Dürrenmatt wants to make us believe that his plot is *not* absurd. He demands of us, for example, that we take Böckmann's death scene seriously. But can one take seriously such a scene in the midst of absurdities? *Frank der Fünfte* is convincing neither as a model of a new world nor as an allegory for our own.

Of course, Dürrenmatt's main concern was not

realism: the musical interludes prove that. They disguise sentiments that could be taken as clichés. For instance, Frank's song on the occasion of Böckmann's death makes even this scene bearable, because now we do not have to take it seriously—in spite of Dürrenmatt's intention. In his Munich speech Dürrenmatt said, "Whoever takes me at my word here will begin to understand what the play really has to say. Whoever fails to understand me in this scene does not understand me at all."[7] The Böckmann scene is not clearly thought through, in spite of the fact that it is impressive; it is built into the wrong play. This scene could be believed in a tragedy—but not in this comedy.

In what way should Böckmann's death be more tragic than that of the others? Why does he see the light only at the last moment? Böckmann is a Catholic; otherwise, he could be exonerated from his sins without actual confession. Since, however, he really repents but is prevented from confessing, his good intention will be taken for the deed. Under these circumstances he could have asked Frank to have a priest come and administer extreme unction after his death. Then a confession would not have been necessary, and Frank would have had no grounds on which to oppose extreme unction. Böckmann would have been assured his place in heaven. The drivel Frank spouts about God's grace is, of course, blasphemous; it is also meaningless, improbable, and impractical.

All the negative criticism notwithstanding, the play has several brilliant scenes, such as the scene before the safe. And the dialogue is sometimes excellent. Häberlin's ideal of the peaceful prison cell, the affairs with the uranium mines and the fire insurance, the parodies of *Hamlet, Macbeth*, Brecht, and Schiller—these are all outstanding details in a comedy that, as a whole, does not succeed.

After the failure of *Frank der Fünfte* Dürrenmatt waited three years before he had his next play produced —*The Physicists*, a comedy in two acts (1962). There is no great difference in the universal skepticism on which both plays are based. In *The Physicists*, the physicist Möbius attempts to keep his discoveries secret by having himself committed to an insane asylum. He knows that the destruction of the world would not be far off if people like Frank VI were to exploit his discoveries politically and economically. But his attempt is of no avail. The doctor in charge of the asylum, a woman with an aristocratic (and criminal) family background (generals, politicians, business leaders), gains possession of his formula and builds up an industrial empire that will give her money and power; it will also annihilate all of humanity and will finally destroy the earth.

In contrast to *Frank der Fünfte, The Physicists* is a clearly conceived and precisely constructed play— Dürrenmatt's best achievement in form. It is also, after *The Visit*, his most successful work. As in *The Visit*, Dürrenmatt lays a "tragedy trap"; here, the audience observes with amusement how three mad men act in an insane asylum. All three have been nuclear physicists. One believes himself to be Newton; the second, Einstein; King Solomon appears regularly to the third. Completely harmless they are not; "Einstein" and "Newton" have each killed a female attendant; at the end of Act I, Möbius kills the third. By the time of the intermission, no spectator yet knows where all this is going to lead. The audience has been well entertained and amused, but it has no inkling that it has just been watching people on whose actions the future of mankind will depend.

In the second act the true situation is revealed. Möbius is not crazy; he has discovered the ultimate truths in physics: the control of gravity and the system behind all possible inventions. He considers his discoveries too dangerous for the hands of unscrupulous politicians, generals, and business leaders. For this reason, he has fled to the insane asylum, where he can work on his formulas in peace. He believes that no one will take him seriously, since he claims that King Solomon (wisdom) inspires him. He is wrong, however; his dissertation had been so promising that the Western and the Eastern powers each send a spy into the asylum—"Einstein" and "Newton." They are supposed either to steal the formulas or to kidnap Möbius or, better still, to talk him into entering the service of their respective governments.

All this becomes clear in the second act, and Möbius convinces both spies (and the audience) that the best thing for humanity would be if all three of them were to remain in the insane asylum. At this point one sees the reason behind the three murders: each attendant had found out that her ward was not crazy at all, had fallen in love with him, and had wanted to marry him. Love had recognized the truth behind the masks and became a threat to the world. The women who loved had to be killed—in the interest of the human race.

In his "21 Punkte zu den *Physikern*" [Twenty-One Points about *The Physicists*], Dürrenmatt writes, "A story has been completely thought through when it has taken its worst possible turn."[8] This happens now, to the physicists' horror: the head doctor, who had seen through the three physicists, drugged Möbius at night and copied his formulas. She has already begun making use of the formulas she holds. The three physicists have sacrificed themselves in vain, and now they are powerless to undertake anything. Since all three have committed murder, they will be kept behind bars from now on and watched by brutal male attendants. There is no one left to prove their normality to, and if they could, they would be put behind bars as murderers. The story has taken its "worst possible turn."

Chance plays an important role in this play. Had Möbius not chanced upon this particular sanatorium, Les Cerisiers (The Cherry Trees), then he would indeed have been able to hide his discoveries from the world. Dürrenmatt was aware of this fact and defended himself in the "21 Punkte" thus: "The worst possible turn is not predictable. It occurs accidentally. The dramatist's art is to integrate chance most effectively into a plot."[9] Dürrenmatt has done this, and one believes Möbius when he claims, "Whatever has been thought of once can never be taken back again."[10]

But chance plays nasty tricks only on the physicists, especially on Möbius. For the doctor, chance is no problem. Once she has Möbius in her hands, she makes elaborate plans for the future. She even places carefully chosen attendants with the "patients," confident in her expectation that they will fall in love with the physicists and subsequently be killed by their lovers. She is so sure of her plans that she gives Möbius's attendant permission to marry him and take him home with her—certain all the while that Möbius will kill her first.

Is Dr. Mathilde von Zahnd really insane? It depends on how she interprets *her* relationship with King Solomon, whom she says is in frequent contact with her. If she is serious, then she is crazy. If she is speaking ironically, parodying Möbius, then she is as normal as her ancestors. Like them, she is out for money and power and does not care whether she ruins the world. It is, of course, a real *coup de théâtre* when it becomes clear at the end that the inmates are normal and the doctor insane. There is, however, another possible interpretation of the play: Dr. von Zahnd is crazy like *all* people; only three are "normal," and these are locked up in an asylum.

The play is constructed along strictly classical lines: the unities of place, time, and action are observed. Much of the second act is an inversion of the first: Act I is comic; in Act II the comic reveals itself to be tragic. Both acts begin with a discussion about smoking. In the first act, the inspector is refused permission to smoke a cigar in the hospital. In the second act, after another murder, Dr. von Zahnd offers him a cigar; but by now the inspector has been so shocked by the events that he refuses to smoke. In the first act the nurse insists that the murder be referred to as an "accident"; by the second act the inspector is persuaded to speak of an "accident," but Dr. von Zahnd now calls it "murder." In the first act, the inspector is perspiring; in the second act the doctor is suffering from imaginary heat. These are just a few examples of the many parallels that link the two parts of the play. When watching the second act, the audience should realize that what had seemed only comic in the first act is now deeply grotesque and disquieting.

The German critic Hans Mayer and others have compared *The Physicists* to Brecht's *Galileo*. Galileo was prepared to recant so that he might continue to work in secret. To him, science was progressive and therefore good. With Dürrenmatt it is just the opposite; scientific discoveries must be retracted because they are too dangerous for men. Fifty years ago, Shaw and some of the German expressionists had foretold what was bound to happen. It was clear to them that technology could not be held back. The only solution to save the world was, in their view, to change the nature of man. Dürrenmatt, a skeptic by nature, with another world war behind him, can no longer take such a possibility seriously.

The first time Dürrenmatt concerned himself with the idea of putting nuclear physicists on the stage was probably in 1956. At that time he discussed Robert Jungk's book, *Heller als tausend Sonnen* [Brighter than a Thousand Suns] in *Weltwoche* (December 7). The book treats Einstein's and Szilard's attempts to induce the American government to put a halt to the development of the atomic bomb—after the war with Germany had ended. This, after Einstein had spurred on speedier construction of the bomb during the war because he feared that Hitler's scientists were working on such a weapon. The United States did not take Einstein's and Szilard's advice; instead, they attempted to keep the research secret—with the result that the Soviet Union began to work on the bomb feverishly.

In his discussion of the Jungk book, Dürrenmatt mentions that as late as 1939 there had been no more than "twelve men, who by mutual agreement" could have prevented the construction of the A-bomb. *The Physicists* is an exact illustration of the following passage from Dürrenmatt's review:

The principle on which the hydrogen bomb is based was discovered by Houtermans, as he considered activity on the sun. Houtermans' misfortune was to live in a world in which a certain type of thinking is obviously as dangerous as smoking in a powder factory. It is, however, impossible to set up as a moral principle the duty to remain a dunce.

The question is what stand physicists, and not only physicists, must take in the world of today. In the future, perhaps, thinking will become more and more dangerous.[11]

One year after *The Physicists*, the comedy *Herkules und der Stall des Augias*, reworked from the radio play, appeared on the stage. In the land of Elis (Switzerland), manure has piled up yards deep. The inhabitants, in a fit of enthusiasm, decide to have their national hero, Hercules, come to clean up all this manure. He plans to wash the mess out into the ocean, with the help of two rivers. But meanwhile the people have been reconsidering things and have reached the conclusion that a life without manure just would not be the same any more; after all, it is really not so bad to live in manure. So they are all happy when the waterworks bureau and the courts refuse permission for the big cleaning. Hercules, with his wife Dejaneira and his secretary, has to move on—unable even to start the job.

The plot unfolds rather slowly. Dürrenmatt parodies the version of the legend given by Gustav Schwab (who wrote popular retellings of the Greek and Roman myths). Hercules is extremely lazy and has had no luck with his first labors. Dejaneira has been a prostitute; only her threats to go back to her old profession force Hercules into action. Hercules hires the farmhand Cambyses to keep happy all the love-crazed females who want to sleep with Hercules. Unrecognized, Cambyses performs his duties in the security of a dark tent. In the stage version, Augias's daughter is after the hero; Dejaneira gets jealous and eventually kills her husband with the shirt of Nessus.

A good part of the humor results from Dürrenmatt's use of dialect expressions (Greek-Swiss names like Pentheus vom Säuliboden). He parodies the national hymn and the dozens of proverbs that one constantly hears in Switzerland ("He who does not . . . harms the homeland"; "the freest folk in the world"; and so forth). The non-Swiss will not understand all of the humor. One would expect that the Swiss audience would savor the really amusing things in each scene; but they are quite sensitive when it comes to matters of patriotism. Although they will concede certain faults, they are convinced that Switzerland is the best possible country in the world.

The comedy was received as a malicious exaggeration. The audience did not laugh; it became angry. In contrast to Frisch, however, Dürrenmatt has hardly ever criticized Switzerland in any concrete way. Except for the various committees, whose function it is to prevent any reforms from taking place in time, very little is mocked directly. The mild, lighthearted mockery is completely invalidated in the garden scene: where Augias lives, the manure has turned into humus. Why not in other places? If Augias is the only one who does things right (he does the best he can in the matters that concern him), why then call in Hercules at all?

As he did after the failure of *Frank der Fünfte*, Dürrenmatt let three years pass before he brought a new play to the stage—*Der Meteor* [The Meteor]. Again it was a comedy, well defined in content and classical in form rules. In *The Physicists* Möbius says, "There is really nothing more offensive than a miracle in the realm of science."[12] In *Der Meteor* Dürrenmatt treats the theme of the miracle with vicious irony. Wolfgang Schwitter, a writer, should have—according to the doctors—died a year ago. Finally, on the longest day of the year, the doctors can confirm Schwitter's death in the hospital. They close his eyes, bind up his jaw, fold his hands, and place candles around him.

Medically, Schwitter is a corpse; but about an hour after his death, he revives, absconds with the candles under his arm, and turns up in the painter's studio where he had begun his career forty years ago—in the hope that here he can die once and for all.

Both acts take place in the studio. A wild farce unfolds here, and the audience laughs until they hurt. Some critics found the whole idea blasphemous; after all, one should not joke about the resurrection and the story of Lazarus. But the whole matter has nothing at all to do with Lazarus and Christ. Bänziger is right when he states, "The catchword 'Lazarus' is just bait for the public *and* the critics."[13]

The medical history of Schwitter is certainly strange. His heart has repeatedly ceased all activity for minutes at a time—and in two instances for almost an hour. Then it started beating again. Other organs, too, were severely damaged. At the examination in Act II they are found to be in perfect condition. In Act I Schwitter dies for short periods six different times. At the beginning of the second act he has been dead for an hour. From then on, however, he stays alive to the end of the play (and beyond).

Medically, Schwitter's case is a riddle, a miracle, an annoyance. The preacher interprets it as a miracle, but he is so little prepared for a real miracle that he has a heart attack. Schwitter is a cynic; he has led an evil life. Such people find no rest after death and must hang around as ghosts; Schwitter is condemned to be a ghost in the flesh. He wishes to die, but he cannot. Where Kafka failed, Schwitter succeeds: he burns his manuscripts. He has realized the meaninglessness of money and burns a million and a half francs in bank notes.

Schwitter, like Korbes in "Incident at Twilight," is in part Dürrenmatt's self-persiflage. Schwitter wants to become a classical writer (*Der Meteor* is built on the three unities); he has "inspirations"; he likes to eat and drink. But greater than the self-parody is the mockery of the critics in Friedrich George's speech at Schwitter's deathbed:

He, who refused to see the tragic side of life, had to die a tragic death. In this dismal light we have to see him—for the first time, perhaps, in uncompromising clarity—as the last despairing man in a time that is readying itself to conquer despair. For him, nothing existed except naked reality. Nevertheless, that was why he thirsted for justice, longed for brotherhood. In vain. Only he who believes in the light side of dark things recognizes that injustice (which also exists in the world) is something unavoidable. He then gives up the struggle and reconciles himself. Schwitter remained unreconciled. He lacked belief in humanity. His morality was grounded in his nihilism. He remained a rebel, a rebel in an airless space. He created because of an inner impasse, not because of a desire to reflect reality. His theater, and not reality, is grotesque. These are his limits. Schwitter remained subjective—in a grand way, to be sure. But his art did not heal; it wounded.[14]

That Schwitter keeps on living has horrifying consequences: the painter breaks his neck; the landlord is arrested as a murderer; Schwitter's wife poisons herself; his doctor is a broken man; and Schwitter's mother-in-law has a heart attack. Some find a falling off in the final scene of Schwitter. Here the formerly cynical Schwitter suddenly speaks seriously; he defends his work and his life and speaks like the author of *Der Blinde* and *Die Stadt*. But here Dürrenmatt does not put the responsibility on God:

I have been called to die; only death is eternal. Life is a rotten business, a dirty trick of nature, an obscene aberration of carbon and oxygen, a malicious cancer on the earth's surface, a scab that never heals. Put together out of dead things, we decompose again into dead things.[15]

These words have too little weight when taken as part of the whole play. They only destroy the comedy momentarily; they are not followed by other tragic elements. In *Der Meteor* there is no "tragedy trap."

The year 1967 brought the production of Dürrenmatt's new version of his first play, *Die Wiedertäufer*. In the following year Dürrenmatt accepted the invitation to become a member of the executive board of the newly organized Basel Theaters (the Stadttheater and the Komödie were placed under common direction). He produced two plays in Basel, with great success: *König Johann* [King John] and *Play Strindberg*.

In the epilogue to *König Johann*, Dürrenmatt claims that Shakespeare's *King John* is a reworking of the anonymous drama *The Troublesome Reign of John King of England*. Some scholars believe that the anonymous play was redone after Shakespeare's drama. Whichever the case might be, Dürrenmatt succeeds with his *König Johann* in taking the anonymous play as his model without doing Shakespeare's version unnecessary violence. Shakespeare's play is patriotic, written for an English public. Dürrenmatt's drama exposes all aspects of power politics and is written for everyone.

The king and the clergymen are big-time gangsters who conceive of the people only as units of manpower; they are prepared to sacrifice the lives of their subjects at the drop of a hat. Each ruler tries to get his hands on as much territory as possible—through marriage, war, betrayal, murder, or religion. To have territories means to have subjects; to have subjects means to have soldiers and income from taxes; to have taxes and soldiers means to have power. On the one hand, the audience is interested in the fate of the individual gangsters on the stage; on the other hand, it is constantly aware that everything happening on the stage has parallels in contemporary politics.

The bastard, Sir Richard, a likable patriot in Shakespeare (where he is called Philip), has now become the voice of reason. He does everything in his power to establish peace, but events prove that chance is stronger than reason, that John would have probably done better by acting unreasonably. Richard is a tragic figure. He betrays his beloved and denies himself personal prosperity in the interest of world peace. But no matter what he does, it turns out wrong. At the end he withdraws from the ruling class to join forces with the common people; the common people must become strong and self-confident enough to annihilate the aristocracy.

This is again a wrong decision: the heads of the modern pseudodemocracies rule no differently from the ancient kings. What determines world history? The ambition of certain mothers, children born at the wrong time, words spoken in the heat of passions. That the bastard Richard was promoted so rapidly proves that the privileges of the nobility are based . . . on nothing! Might makes right. The people are always betrayed. The citizens of Angers have three possibilities. If they declare themselves for Arthur, then they will be destroyed by John. If they declare themselves for John, then Philip, the French king, will be on their backs. They choose neutrality and are destroyed by John *and* Philip. The kings are monsters. John betrays his own mother, and Philip kills her so that John will be forced to murder the eight-year-old Arthur. There are no ethical principles; each murder may be carried out in God's name—as long as the murder is useful to the church.

What was serious in Shakespeare is now intentionally exaggerated to the point of comedy. The play is full of farcical humor (especially in the characters of Leopold of Austria and the papal legate). In one place, however, Dürrenmatt speaks seriously: in the first scene of the third act John suddenly turns into a premature Luther and attacks the Catholic Church for selling indulgences. In this scene even Philip speaks with more insight than one would have given him credit for.

In Shakespeare's play King John's son suddenly turns up as a *deus ex machina*: the audience had not even known that he existed. Dürrenmatt integrates him more legitimately into the action, as a newborn baby. In Shakespeare, John is poisoned by a monk; in Dürrenmatt, Pembroke performs this task. In Shakespeare's play the Bastard renounces his right to succession in favor of John's son. In Dürrenmatt, Richard is flogged by his former beloved and leaves the court.

Play Strindberg, first performed in Basel on February 8, 1969, is Dürrenmatt's version of Strindberg's *The Dance of Death*. It was wise of Dürrenmatt not to use the same title, because the two plays do not have much in common. Nestroy's Tannhäuser parody is amusing and is not detrimental to Wagner's opera. One might say the same of *Play Strindberg*: the play is grotesque and funny and does not debase *The Dance of Death*. Strindberg has as little need for rewriting as Dürrenmatt, but the latter had to justify his new version in some way; so he scornfully called Strindberg's play "literature" and "stuffy." Some critics immediately went along with Dürrenmatt's opinion; they may be well advised to read *The Dance of Death* more closely. Strindberg's hell is considerably deeper and hotter than Dürrenmatt's. *Play Strindberg* is, however, not watered-down Strindberg but rather a new play—grotesque, diabolical, comical—typically Dürrenmatt in style.

One would think that the portrayal of a twelve-round fight between a husband and wife would have appealed more to Frisch than to Dürrenmatt. Frisch's *Die grosse Wut des Philipp Hotz* [The Great Rage of Philip Hotz] contains, however, only the equivalent of Dürrenmatt's first two or three rounds. Common to both these Swiss authors is the outcome: the women are victorious.

In Strindberg's play there is still some love hidden behind all the hate. One understands, too, just how this hate has come to exist. In Dürrenmatt's gruesome brawl, the people hate without reason, just as naturally as cats hate dogs. The third person in both plays is Kurt, who, in Strindberg's work, is drawn into the fight against his will. He is seduced by the woman but finally breaks away in order not to become completely inhuman. Dürrenmatt makes Kurt a rich American gangster who feels right at home in the milieu of ruthless throat-cutting. Strindberg presents life as a mystery; in *Play Strindberg* it is a terrible absurdity.

7

Dürrenmatt at Fifty

In 1969, Dürrenmatt published an expanded version of a paper he had read at the University of Mainz: "Monstervortrag über Gerechtigkeit und Recht. Nebst einem helvetischen Zwischenspiel" [Huge Speech on Justice and on Law. With a Swiss Interlude]. The subtitle was "Eine kleine Dramaturgie der Politik" [A Short Dramaturgy About Politics]. Dürrenmatt starts out with an anecdote about three Arabs and uses it to demonstrate the complexity of the term "justice." The interlude is witty: innocent Switzerland is shown to be, in fact, a wolf clothed in a lamb's coat. The long speech closes with a hilarious story about Harun al Raschid. This work proves that Dürrenmatt is still pondering human and divine justice. He has come to the conclusion that the term "justice," in fact, can mean everything and nothing. Its value is so questionable that one must ignore it. If one does not expect justice, then he will not have to be disillusioned.

In the same year Dürrenmatt traveled to the United States to accept an honorary doctorate at Temple University in Philadelphia. From there he traveled to Florida, Mexico, Jamaica, and Puerto Rico. In Puerto Rico his money was stolen. Probably to balance the loss, he published a little book, *Sätze aus Amerika* [Sentences from America, 1970]. The contents of the whole book could have been printed on a few pages of a periodical. The text contains a short account of Dürrenmatt's trip and a collection of aphorisms that came to his mind while on the other side of the Atlantic. One learns that Dürrenmatt is working on a novel—*Der Pensionierte* [The Pensioner]. The outline Dürrenmatt gives indicates that the premise of the novel will be the bringing together by a retired judge of all those whom he had not sentenced, although they had been technically guilty enough. He had spared them because he had found them to be innocent victims of their milieu. The plot reminds one of Agatha Christie's *And Then There Were None*, where another retired judge succeeds in killing those murderers he had not been able to convict legally.

Also in 1969 Dürrenmatt resigned his directorship of the Basel Theaters in protest. His next play, an adaption of Goethe's *Urfaust* (the original *Faust*) was staged in Zurich in October, 1970. Dürrenmatt mixed three elements together: Goethe's text, the text of the anonymous Faust book of 1587, and his own inventions. The action proceeds rapidly; scene follows scene; the actors double as stagehands and stay right on the stage to the end of the play. Mephistopheles has become a comic figure, a master of gags; Faust is no longer a vital and ambitious young man but an old codger who succeeds in seducing the child Gretchen. Dürrenmatt's piece is original, full of new ideas and shocking gags. The public was highly amused; the critics had mixed feelings.

Dürrenmatt's most recent original play, *Portrait eines Planeten* [Portrait of a Planet], first performed in Düsseldorf on November 10, 1970, was very negatively received by the press. If one considers the philosophies behind *Die Stadt, An Angel Comes to Babylon*, "Das Unternehmen der Wega," and *The Physicists*, one must come to the conclusion that Dürrenmatt will, one day, write a successful play in which he demonstrates how ridiculous (and dangerous) the human situation on Earth really is. What is the role of the little planet Earth in the context of the universe? Our planet, evidently, is of no importance whatever. And what is the importance of a human being on this little, unimportant planet? Nil! We have no guarantee that our existence will continue for even a week. At any time, the sun may explode, change into a supernova, and terminate life on this planet.

This is what happens in *Portrait eines Planeten*. Four women and four men act in twenty-five scenes that offer a summary of the history of humanity since the time of cannibalism. One is an artist; the second, a commander of a concentration camp; the third, a politician; the fourth, a physicist. The scenes take place in Vietnam, in a conference room, among the hippies, in a space ship. Then the sun explodes and puts an end to all these absurd happenings. The German critic Hans Schwab-Felisch has called the play a *Kosmisches Kabarett* (cosmological literary cabaret); and this is exactly what it is. Dürrenmatt staged a revised version of this cabaret about the end of the world in Zurich (April, 1971). This time the reaction of the critics was better. But Dürrenmatt is at this point still hesitant about publishing the text.

I have mentioned that Dürrenmatt saw Peter Brook's production of *Titus Andronicus* in Paris and that this had given him the inspiration to write *Frank der Fünfte*. In 1970 Dürrenmatt made up his mind to adapt Shakespeare directly. *Titus Andronicus: Nach Shakespeare* was staged in Düsseldorf on December 12, 1970.

There is no doubt about who is good and who is bad in Shakespeare's play. The Moor Aaron is a wicked devil whose soul is as black as his skin. He is openly pleased about every crime he can inspire others to commit or can commit himself. The princess Tamora is almost as bad as Aaron. Since one of her sons is killed she has a motive to murder the family of Andronicus. But she would have committed murder anyhow. She has no heart; she deceives her husband, the emperor of

Rome, commits adultery with Aaron, and gives birth to a black child. Shakespeare's London public sympathized with the Romans. For the Elizabethans, all non-Europeans were bad (and inferior). Therefore, most of the audience would be expected to take Titus's side. Indeed, in some ways, Titus is an early version of King Lear.

In the course of the play, about twenty persons (most of the characters) are killed on stage. Titus loses his hands, and his daughter is raped; she also loses a hand and her tongue. Nevertheless, Shakespeare's play is not a tragedy. One of Titus's twenty-five sons succeeds in surviving and manages to become emperor of Rome in the end. Shakespeare's public went home content. The killings were quickly forgotten; they did not really matter, just as we don't care about the killings in a novel by Mickey Spillane. The gangsters are not really lifelike; they are figures in a chess game. As long as the tough detective survives, the reader is happy.

But the literary public of today seems to be considerably more "sensitive" than in Shakespeare's time. If a murderer is to be hanged, thousands of women demonstrate against the death penalty. If a guerrilla is shot in Latin America, American students protest in front of some consulate. If a member of the Mafia is killed in Sicily, the press is shocked about the cruelty of the Italian police. For many people today, no black can do any wrong. Dürrenmatt seems to have shared this modern belief. In his play Aaron is a decent man; no trace of the demonic is left.

Dürrenmatt has added one person to the dramatis personae of Shakespeare's play—Alaric, king of the Visigoths. The successive killings are interrupted by discussions about Dürrenmatt's favorite topics, including piety. The Visigoths have killed a few of Titus's

sons, and so Titus condemns one of Tamora's sons to
death. Tamora asks for mercy, but Titus replies self-
righteously, "Grace is reserved for the pious!"[1] Dürrenmatt's Titus is a hypocrite. He does not act as a true
Christian should, and he will be punished for his false
piety. The Visigoths will take their revenge and kill
Titus's other sons. Dürrenmatt, of course, did not want
to say this, but the developments in the play support the
conclusion that it would have been best if Titus had
reacted unscrupulously and had killed all the Visigoths
when he had the chance (at the beginning of the play).
In that case, no Romans would have been killed later
on, and peace and happiness would have reigned every-
where.

After "piety," Titus introduces the term "justice"
for discussion. Titus is of the same opinion as Romulus:

> Rome's greatness is not the sword, it is
> The law by which it governs the world.
> If this law is allowed to break down, then Rome has
>   lost the right
> To subject other people to this law.[2]

When Titus's son Mutius wants to prevent his father
from marrying his sister Lavinia off to the emperor
(she loves Bassianus, the brother of the emperor, and is
already engaged to him), Mutius is killed by his own
father because "he stands in the way" of what Titus
considers to be Rome's law. After Mutius is dead, it
turns out that the emperor Saturninus did not want to
marry Lavinia anyhow; he marries Tamora. The killing
had been absolutely pointless. Saturninus has Titus
"pensioned."

To turn Aaron into a good man, Dürrenmatt had

to invent a psychologically convincing background for him. The clichés are horrifying: Aaron had lived happily in Africa when the slave hunters caught him; he was sold to a white general; the general and his wife enjoyed Aaron's beautiful body; Aaron became a male prostitute; he was so successful and appreciated that he ended up as Tamora's friend. The few doubtful traits in his character are therefore explained and excused. No black spectator can now possibly feel offended.

In Shakespeare's play, Aaron deceives Titus into cutting off his hands. To relieve Aaron of such a black deed, Dürrenmatt introduces a white hangman who talks Titus into mutilating himself. Titus's sacrifice is to no avail: the Goths kill two of his sons and carry their heads onto the stage. At this point, finally, Titus makes up his mind to take revenge. In order to protect himself he pretends to have become insane:

> The absurdity
> Of the world can only be conquered by madness.[3]

Dürrenmatt's fourth scene has no parallel in Shakespeare's play. Lucius, the last surviving son of Titus, goes to see Alaric and offers to help him in conquering Rome and killing Saturninus. Meanwhile, Tamora gives birth to a black child; Aaron intends to return to Africa with his son. Titus organizes the last supper to which he invites everybody of importance. Titus speaks of "justice," which has been "lost," and plans to kill all his enemies. In Shakespeare's play, Titus's brother escapes with his life; Dürrenmatt has him hanged. The sixteenth-century Aaron kills two midwives; the twentieth-century Aaron, only one.

In the end, the following characters are dead: the emperor Saturninus and his brother; the princess Ta-

mora and all her sons; Aaron; Titus Andronicus, with
his brother and all his sons except for Lucius; Lavinia;
a midwife; and a farmer. The audience has also wit-
nessed the cutting off of several hands, the cutting out
of a tongue, the chopping off of two heads, and a rape.
In addition, it has watched Tamora eating her two sons
in the form of a meat pie. Alaric speaks the final words.
He knows that his reign will only last a short while. He
and his Visigoths will be followed by the Huns, the
Turks, the Mongols. Under these circumstances, he is
totally cynical:

> What's the use of "justice," what's the use of
>   "revenge"?
> These are just words, evil humbug!
> The balloon Earth—it is driven through emptiness
> And it will die as we are bound to die—to no
>   purpose.
> Everything that was, is, and will be must perish.[4]

The first performance of Dürrenmatt's *Titus Andronicus* was a sensation. The continuous killings, bury-
ings, and mutilations were too much for the Düsseldorf
audience. They did not know that all these happenings
already were done by Shakespeare. They considered
Dürrenmatt a sadist with a perverse pleasure in bringing their dinners up from the stomach. When Titus cut
his hands off, part of the audience walked out. Some
critics were horrified and called the action of the play
"a pointless and unending slaughter on stage." But even
those critics who knew Shakespeare's play were not
enthusiastic. Why did Dürrenmatt have to change
Shakespeare's text at all? Why should he discuss piety
and justice once more? After all, we have heard all this
before. So life on this planet is absurd. Evidently,

Shakespeare had thought so, too. Then why water down the Elizabethan's text?

In 1971, Dürrenmatt celebrated his fiftieth birthday. On this occasion, the Zurich Schauspielhaus [Playhouse] organized a special matinee performance. Seventeen actors read published and unpublished scripts by Dürrenmatt. At the age of fifty, he is the most successful dramatist who writes in German; the most frequently performed play in 1970 was *Play Strindberg*: 696 performances at thirty-three German-speaking theaters, before 222,000 spectators.

In early 1971, people expected the publication of *Urfaust* and *Portrait eines Planeten*. Instead, a short novel appeared—*Der Sturz*, Dürrenmatt's first novel since 1958 (*The Pledge*). In this story the ministers in a government are numbered from A to P. This government is supposed to be a model for all possible systems in all possible institutions (state, factory, library, university). False rumor and chance are responsible for a reorganization of the party hierarchy: A, the president, is killed; D becomes his successor. Some of the others move up. The reason for this exemplary inside revolution is fear. Since O does not appear at the meeting, the others fear that he has been removed by A. Since he was close to some members of the party hierarchy, these members begin to fear that they will be next on the list. Indeed they are. O, however, was not removed; he had mixed up the date of the meeting. When he finally arrives, A is already dead.

Dürrenmatt presents a parable—similar to one used by H. J. C. von Grimmelshausen in the great seventeenth-century German novel *Simplicius Simplicissimus* —in which all human beings are given a position in relation to a tree; the ones near the top move higher and higher—until they fall down. Dürrenmatt's model reminds the reader of a Russian, Chinese, or East German top-level meeting of the Communist Party. Few will believe that such an action could take place in a Western country. The fact that Dürrenmatt introduces an English lord will deceive nobody. Whether Dürrenmatt intended to or not, he has written an anticommunist pamphlet.

It is probable that Dürrenmatt still has much to offer. What he has achieved up to now, however, would be enough for us to consider him among the more important dramatists of German (and world) literature. Besides obvious genius, Dürrenmatt possesses the characteristics that distinguished Shaw: a sharp critical intelligence and the honesty to think through a problem logically and uncompromisingly (even when the end is despair). Dürrenmatt has the background of a great humanist. He also has a vital and indestructible sense of humor, which encompasses everything from crude puns to grotesque absurdities, and includes satire as well as the most polished parody.

Dürrenmatt is convinced of the absurdity of human existence; isolated man stands powerless, facing the void. The human race is digging its own grave because of its senseless worship of technology. Even if Dürrenmatt, with his hard logic, is far from being a devout Christian, many of his works are like sermons. They contain hidden challenges to act like Bärlach and not like the inhabitants of Güllen. They ask us to distrust slogans and shibboleths and any kind of political leadership.

Notes

1. The Horror Lurking Behind the Scenes

1. Friedrich Dürrenmatt, *Theater-Schriften und Reden* (Zurich: Arche, 1966), p. 30.
2. J. Howald, *Ulrich Dürrenmatt und seine Gedichte* (Meiringen: Walter Loepthien Verlag, 1926), Vol. I, p. 153.
3. Friedrich Dürrenmatt, *Die Stadt* (Zurich: Arche, 1952), p. 151.
4. Hans Bänziger, *Frisch und Dürrenmatt*, 5th ed. (Bern: Francke, 1967), p. 126.
5. Dürrenmatt, *Die Stadt*, pp. 197–98.
6. Ibid., p. 11.
7. Ibid., p. 16.
8. Ibid., p. 20.
9. Ibid., p. 20.
10. Elisabeth Brock-Sulzer, *Friedrich Dürrenmatt: Stationen seines Werkes* (Zurich: Arche, 1960), p. 124.
11. Dürrenmatt, *Die Stadt*, p. 167.

12. Ibid., p. 172.
13. Ibid., p. 174.

2. *The Early Dramas*

1. Friedrich Dürrenmatt, *Komödien II und Frühe Stücke* (Zurich: Arche, 1963), p. 115.
2. Elisabeth Brock-Sulzer, *Friedrich Dürrenmatt: Stationen seines Werkes* (Zurich: Arche, 1960), p. 19.
3. Dürrenmatt, *Komödien II*, p. 114.
4. Ibid., p. 114.
5. Ibid., pp. 12–13.
6. Beda Allemann, *"Es steht geschrieben"* in *Das deutsche Drama*, ed. Benno von Wiese (Düsseldorf: Bagel, 1958), Vol. II, p. 418. The quotes on the following lines are taken from the subsequent pages in Allemann's essay.
7. Dürrenmatt, *Komödien II*, p. 48.
8. Ibid., p. 66.
9. Friedrich Dürrenmatt, *Die Wiedertäufer* (Zurich: Arche, 1967), p. 109.
10. Ibid., p. 94.
11. Ibid., p. 94.
12. Ibid., p. 95.
13. Ibid., p. 37.
14. The quotes in this paragraph are from Dürrenmatt, *Komödien II*, pp. 142–49.
15. Ibid., p. 167.
16. Ibid., p. 168.
17. Ibid., p. 170.
18. Ibid., p. 190.
19. Ibid., p. 191.

3. *From* Romulus *to* The Visit

1. Friedrich Dürrenmatt, *Komödien I* (Zurich: Arche, 1957), p. 19.

2. Ibid., p. 60.
3. Ibid., p. 54.
4. Hans Bänziger, *Frisch und Dürrenmatt*, 5th ed. (Bern: Francke, 1967), p. 145.
5. Friedrich Dürrenmatt: *Die Ehe des Herrn Mississippi: Bühnenfassung und Drehbuch* (Zurich: Arche, 1966), p. 87.
6. Ibid., p. 38.
7. Ibid., p. 136.
8. Dürrenmatt, *Komödien I*, p. 217.
9. Ibid., p. 199.
10. Elisabeth Brock-Sulzer, *Friedrich Dürrenmatt: Stationen seines Werkes* (Zurich: Arche, 1960), p. 51.
11. Dürrenmatt, *Komödien I*, p. 318.

4. Four Detective Stories and a Comic Novel

1. Friedrich Dürrenmatt, *Der Verdacht*, 3rd ed. (Einsiedeln: Benziger, 1960), p. 50.
2. Ibid., p. 106.
3. Ibid., p. 109.
4. Ibid., p. 138.
5. Ibid., p. 142.
6. Friedrich Dürrenmatt, *Das Versprechen*, 3rd ed. (Zurich: Arche, 1958), p. 19.
7. Ibid., p. 18.
8. Ibid., p. 51.
9. Ibid., p. 138.
10. Dürrenmatt, *Der Verdacht*, p. 21.
11. Friedrich Dürrenmatt, *Die Panne/Der Tunnel*, ed. F. J. Alexander (Oxford: Oxford University Press, 1967), p. 38.
12. Friedrich Dürrenmatt, *Grieche sucht Griechin* (Berlin: Ullstein, 1963), p. 137.

5. Radio Plays

1. Friedrich Dürrenmatt, *Gesammelte Hörspiele* (Zurich: Arche, 1961), pp. 15–16.
2. Ibid., p. 35.
3. Ibid., pp. 35–36.
4. Ibid., p. 37.
5. Friedrich Dürrenmatt, *Theater-Schriften und Reden* (Zurich: Arche, 1966), p. 300.
6. Dürrenmatt, *Gesammelte Hörspiele*, p. 106.
7. Ibid., pp. 108–9.
8. Ibid., p. 110.
9. Ibid., p. 211.
10. Ibid., p. 300.
11. Ibid., p. 316.

6. The Absurdity of Human Behavior

1. Horst Bienek, *Werkstattgespräche mit Schriftstellern* (Munich: Deutscher Taschenbuch Verlag, 1965), p. 126.
2. Ibid., p. 126.
3. Friedrich Dürrenmatt, *Komödien II und Frühe Stücke* (Zurich: Arche, 1963), p. 273.
4. Friedrich Dürrenmatt, *Theater-Schriften und Reden* (Zurich: Arche, 1966), p. 190.
5. Ibid., p. 349.
6. Ibid., p. 97.
7. Ibid., p. 352.
8. Ibid., p. 193.
9. Ibid., p. 193.
10. Dürrenmatt, *Komödien II*, p. 350.
11. Dürrenmatt, *Theater-Schriften und Reden*, p. 275.
12. Dürrenmatt, *Komödien II*, p. 317.
13. Hans Bänziger, *Frisch und Dürrenmatt*, 5th ed. (Bern: Francke, 1967), p. 194.

14. Friedrich Dürrenmatt, *Der Meteor* (Zurich: Arche, 1966), p. 41.
15. Ibid., p. 70.

7. *Dürrenmatt at Fifty*

1. Friedrich Dürrenmatt: *Titus Andronicus* (Zurich: Arche, 1970), p. 9.
2. Ibid., p. 12.
3. Ibid., p. 44.
4. Ibid., p. 79.

Bibliography

Works by Friedrich Dürrenmatt

NOTE: Plays, radio plays, and fiction are listed chronologically within each section. The date in brackets indicates the approximate year of composition.

COLLECTED EDITIONS

Komödien I. Zurich: Arche, 1957. (Contains *Romulus der Grosse, Die Ehe des Herrn Mississippi, Ein Engel kommt nach Babylon, Der Besuch der alten Dame.*)

Komödien II und frühe Stücke. Zurich: Arche, 1964. (Contains *Es steht geschrieben, Der Blinde, Frank der Fünfte, Die Physiker, Herkules und der Stall des Augias.*)

Gesammelte Hörspiele. Zurich: Arche, 1961. (Contains "Der Doppelgänger," "Der Prozess um des Esels Schatten," "Nächtliches Gespräch mit einem verachteten Menschen," "Stranitzky und der Nationalheld," "Herkules und der Stall des Augias," "Das Unternehmen der Wega," "Die Panne," "Abendstunde im Spätherbst.")

Theater-Schriften und Reden. Edited by Elisabeth Brock-

107

Sulzer. Zurich: Arche, 1966. (Contains the collected essays, speeches, reviews, and so forth, through 1966.)

PLAYS

Es steht geschrieben [1946]. Basel: Schwabe, 1947. Revised version—Zurich: Arche, 1959.

Der Blinde [1947]. Zurich: Arche, 1960.

Romulus der Grosse [1948]. Zurich: Arche, 1958. Fourth version—Zurich: Arche, 1964.

Die Ehe des Herrn Mississippi [1950]. Zurich: Oprecht, 1952. Final version and screenplay—Zurich: Arche, 1966.

Ein Engel kommt nach Babylon [1953]. Zurich: Arche, 1954.

Der Besuch der alten Dame [1955]. Zurich: Arche, 1956.

Frank der Fünfte [1958]. Zurich: Arche, 1960.

Die Physiker [1961]. Zurich: Arche, 1962.

Herkules und der Stall des Augias [1962 (radio play—1954)]. Zurich: Arche, 1963.

Der Meteor [1964]. Zurich: Arche, 1966.

Die Wiedertäufer [1967]. Zurich: Arche, 1967.

König Johann: Nach Shakespeare [1968]. Zurich: Arche, 1968.

Play Strindberg [1968]. Zurich: Arche, 1969.

Titus Andronicus: Nach Shakespeare [1969]. Zurich: Arche, 1970.

(Not yet published: *Urfaust* [1970]; *Portrait eines Planeten* [1970].)

RADIO PLAYS

"Der Doppelgänger" [1946]. Zurich: Arche, 1960.

"Der Prozess um des Esels Schatten" [1951]. Zurich: Arche, 1956.

"Nächtliches Gespräch mit einem verachteten Menschen" [1952]. Zurich: Arche, 1957.

"Stranitzky und der Nationalheld" [1952]. Zurich: Arche, 1959.

"Herkules und der Stall des Augias" [1954]. Zurich: Arche, 1954.

"Das Unternehmen der Wega" [1954]. Zurich: Arche, 1958.

"Abendstunde im Spätherbst" [1956]. Zurich: Arche, 1959.

"Die Panne" [1961 (narrative version—1956)]. Zurich: Arche, 1961.

FICTION

Die Stadt: Prosa I–IV [1943–52]. Zurich: Arche, 1952.

Der Richter und sein Henker [1950]. Einsiedeln: Benziger, 1952.

Der Verdacht [1951]. Einsiedeln: Benziger, 1951.

Grieche sucht Griechin [1955]. Zurich: Arche, 1955.

Die Panne [1956]. Zurich: Arche, 1956.

Das Versprechen [1957]. Zurich: Arche, 1958.

Der Sturz [1970]. Zurich: Arche, 1971.

MISCELLANEOUS

Die Heimat im Plakat [1963]. Zurich: Diogenes, 1963. (A book of cartoons mainly about the water pollution in Zermatt.)

Monstervortrag über Gerechtigkeit und Recht: Nebst einem helvetischen Zwischenspiel [1968]. Zurich: Arche, 1969.

Sätze aus Amerika [1969]. Zurich: Arche, 1970.

SELECTED ENGLISH TRANSLATIONS

An Angel Comes to Bablyon & Romulus the Great. Translated by William McElwee (*Angel*) and Gerhard Nellhaus (*Romulus*). New York: Grove, 1966.

Four Plays. Translated by Gerhard Nellhaus et al. New York: Grove, 1965. (Contains "Problems of the Theatre," *Romulus the Great, The Marriage of Mr. Mississippi, An Angel Comes to Babylon, The Physicists.*)

"Incident at Twilight." Translated by George E. Wellwarth. In Michael Benedikt and George B. Wellwarth, eds.

Postwar German Theatre. New York: Dutton, 1967.

The Judge and His Hangman. Translated by Therese Pol. New York: Berkley, 1955.

Once a Greek. Translated by Richard and Clara Winston. New York: Knopf, 1965.

The Physicists. Translated by James Kirkup. New York: Grove, 1964.

The Pledge. Translated by Richard and Clara Winston. New York: New American Library, 1960.

Problems of the Theatre, an Essay, and The Marriage of Mr. Mississippi, a Play. Translated by Gerhard Nellhaus ("Problems") and Michael Bullock (*Marriage*). New York: Grove, 1966.

The Quarry. Translated by Eva Morreale. New York: Grove, 1962.

Romulus the Great. New York: Grove, 1966. (Contains Gore Vidal's adaptation and the original Dürrenmatt play in Gerhard Nellhaus's translation.)

Traps. Translated by Richard and Clara Winston. New York: Knopf, 1960.

The Visit. Translated by Patrick Bowles. New York: Grove, 1962.

Works about Friedrich Dürrenmatt

BOOKS

Bänziger, Hans. *Frisch und Dürrenmatt*. 5th ed. Bern: Francke, 1967.

Brock-Sulzer, Elisabeth. *Friedrich Dürrenmatt: Station seines Werkes*. 3rd ed. Zurich: Arche, 1970.

————. *Dürrenmatt in unserer Zeit: Eine Werkinterpretation nach Selbstzeugnissen*. Basel: Reinhardt, 1968.

Der unbequeme Dürrenmatt. Basel: Basilius Presse, 1962. (Essays by Willy Jäggi, Werner Oberle, Gottfried Benn, Fritz Buri, Reinhold Grimm, Hans Mayer, and Elisabeth Brock-Sulzer.)

Hansel, Johannes. *Friedrich-Dürrenmatt-Bibliographie.* Bad Homburg: Gehlen, 1968. (Lists the primary and secondary literature up to 1968, including translations into English and other languages.)

Jauslin, Christian M. *Friedrich Dürrenmatt: Zur Struktur seiner Dramen.* Zurich: Juris, 1964.

Jenny, Urs. *Dürrenmatt.* Velber bei Hannover: Friedrich, 1965.

Mayer, Hans. *Dürrenmatt und Frisch (Anmerkungen).* Pfullingen: Neske, 1963.

Peppard, Murray B. *Friedrich Dürrenmatt.* New York: Twayne, 1969.

Schneider, Peter. *Die Fragwürdigkeit des Rechts im Werk von Friedrich Dürrenmatt.* Karlsruhe: C. F. Müller, 1967.

Strelka, Joseph. *Brecht, Horvath, Dürrenmatt.* Vienna: Forum, 1962.

Syberberg, Hans-Jürgen. *Interpretationen zum Drama Friedrich Dürrenmatts.* Munich: UNI-Druck, 1965.

ESSAYS IN BOOKS AND PERIODICALS

NOTE: The bibliography in Murray B. Peppard's book contains a list of articles in English. Hansel's *Dürrenmatt-Bibliographie* contains several hundred items of secondary literature. The following items have directly influenced this book.

Allemann, Beda. *"Es steht geschrieben."* In Benno von Wiese, ed. *Das deutsche Drama.* Düsseldorf: Bagel, 1958, Vol. II.

Arnold, Armin. "Friedrich Dürrenmatt and Mark Twain." *Proceedings of the Fourth Congress of the International Comparative Literature Association* (Den Haag: Mouton, 1966). II: 1097–1104.

Bienek, Horst. Interview with Dürrenmatt. In *Werkstattgespräche mit Schriftstellern.* Munich: Deutscher Taschenbuch Verlag, 1965.

Pestalozzi, Karl. "F. D." In Wolfgang Rothe, ed. *Deutsche Literatur im 20. Jahrhundert*. Bern: Francke, 1967.

Steiner, Jacob. "Die Komödie Dürrenmatts. *Der Deutschunterricht* 15 (1963), 81–89.

Index

113